Presented To:

D1400266

From:

Date:

ENDORSEMENTS

If you're like me, you've wondered how you—a good Christian—can have so much interference from the devil when you're born again and sold out to God. Well, if you're a believer or not quite a believer yet, this book is what you need. Deliverance is not only necessary for God's people, but it's also an essential tool for all believers. Mark 16:17 says, "And these signs shall follow them that believe; in my name shall they cast out devils." We're in a season when God is releasing multitudes of people who've been trained to help you in deliverance. Dr. John Veal is one of those people. This book is perfect because instructions for you will come in the form of amazing and supernatural stories from the heart and life of the author. Devour this book so you can devour the enemy, Satan, in your life. And while you're at it, get an extra copy of this book for a friend. They *will* thank you!

—STEVE SHULTZ
Founder, The Elijah List

Supernaturally Delivered is fully loaded with keys of deliverance that every Spirit-filled believer needs in their spiritual warfare arsenal to overcome unfortunate circumstances and demonic opposition that hinders and blocks total freedom in Christ to live victorious. Dr. John Veal shares jaw-dropping, eye-opening, and heartfelt personal testimonies and supernatural encounters as it pertains to deliverance ministry in today's society and church community.

Supernaturally Delivered is a comprehensive and practical study guide for those called to be equipped, educated, empowered, and trained with the proper tools in the areas of deliverance and spiritual warfare to become effective deliverance workers. Deliverance is the children's bread, and this powerful, easy-to-read book will stir an appetite within you to receive fresh manna from heaven to give to those who are in dire need of supernatural awakening and spiritual cleaning.

I highly recommend this biblically sound book for the mature and for those ready to destroy the works of darkness with the light of God's kingdom to ultimately see the greatest outcome of people being supernaturally delivered by the power and love of God!

—DR. HAKEEM COLLINS
Champions International
Author of *Heaven Declares, Prophetic Breakthrough*, and *Command Your Healing*

I thank God for Dr. John Veal, who is an amazing vessel in the body of Christ. There are not enough books written on the topic of deliverance that would help bring understanding to the average believer. This book that Pastor Veal has written will help instruct you in how to be self-delivered as well as how to administer deliverance to others who may be in desperate need of freedom and wholeness.

This deliverance manual you're reading will literally activate you in the ministry of deliverance, which is desperately needed in the body of Christ today more now than ever!

Dr. Veal has poured his heart into this book, and it will equip you and bring awareness to you so you may shut down gates, portals, and spirit doors of the demonic realm and keep them from operating in and through your life and the lives of those you hold dear to your heart. I pray that the words of this book would help you in every way. Allow them to germinate within your heart and mind.

—DR. LUIS LOPEZ JR.
Author, *The Counterfeit Christian*
Rochester, NY

Supernaturally Delivered—a powerful and practical publication—gives us fresh and comprehensive insight into the demonic realm and its dark and very subtle activity. The real-life experiences of John Veal authenticate the reality of the enemy's workings, and this book provides pertinent principles and keys to supernaturally securing our freedom from demonic oppression. It's eye-opening to know how spirits infiltrate our lives in the most inconspicuous ways!

As you glean from the pages of this book, do not be alarmed or frightened by the information and enlightenment given. John Veal gives not only a very candid perspective of demonic activity in one's life, but also a clear path to freedom by arming you with the keys to be supernaturally delivered and live in consistent victory! Just as demonic oppression is supernatural, true deliverance is supernatural also! Thank you, John Veal, for such a powerful and practical book!

—Apostle Lorenzo Irving
Author, *Maintaining Your Deliverance* and
The Anointing Is Not Enough
Senior Leader, Life Center Church of Deliverance, Chicago, IL

Dr. Veal releases in-depth and on-time knowledge and wisdom in his book *Supernaturally Delivered*. As a prophetic deliverance minister, I believe he addresses the two most important questions in deliverance ministry: can a Christian have a demon, and should we consult with and ask demons for information?

Prophet Veal not only goes deep in defining spiritual names and definitions, but also gives you practical application through true life experiences to make you ponder and discern if a particular demonic entity could be attacking you.

People perish for lack of knowledge (Hos. 4:6). As you read this book, you will no longer be ignorant of the enemy's devices, but the devil and his cohorts will be exposed and revealed. Be empowered and filled with a new spiritual warfare arsenal through this book on deliverance.

—APOSTLE KATHY DEGRAW
Author, *Discerning and Destroying the Works of Satan*
Founder, DeGraw Ministries and Ruach Ha'Kodesh AEC
www.degrawministries.org

We are living in a time of intense spiritual warfare. There is a battle between the kingdom of light (Jesus) and the kingdom of darkness (Satan). It is imperative to understand the strategies and snares of the enemy.

In his book, *Supernaturally Delivered*, Prophet John Veal teaches you how to recognize the satanic realm. You will understand why there are repercussions for engaging in certain activities that you may think are innocent. He gives a clear perspective on deliverance with discernment from the Holy Spirit. He explains how even believers have opened doors to the demonic realm. He teaches from experience as well as having an ear to hear the voice of God.

I recommend this book for those who know someone in a constant battle or those of you who desire to live a life of freedom and walk in the covenant Jesus has provided for you.

—ELAINE TAVOLACCI
A Word in Season
www.awordinseason.info
www.TheVoiceOfBreakthrough.com
www.TheVoiceOfProphecy.com
www.ElaineTavolacci.com

In this powerful, practical, and transparent book, you will learn the biblical keys to experiencing deliverance and ministering deliverance to others. You will understand the insidious nature of rejection, how it opens the doors to bondage, and how to break free from its harmful grasp. Through his thought-provoking candor, Prophet John Veal leads the reader into the place called freedom and helps equip them to lead others out of their captivity. You will be challenged, and you will be changed!

—Dr. Kynan Bridges
Best-selling Author, *The Power of Prophetic Prayer*
Senior Pastor, Grace and Peace Global Fellowship, Inc.
www.graceempowered.org

The Lord is raising up an army of gospel warriors in this hour. Sons and daughters of God who are heralding the message of salvation, freedom, and deliverance. The fivefold ministers aren't the only ones radically obeying the Great Commission, but every saint of God is taking up the mantle of Jesus Christ and taking it to their neighbors, as well as the nations.

Seasoned prophet, John Veal, is one of those warriors doing a tremendous job of equipping the body of Christ in the gifts of the Spirit and deliverance ministry. He's been doing this for years and has witnessed the hand of God moving in miraculous ways. I believe strongly in the ministry of John Veal, and I know this book will enlighten, encourage, and provoke you to good works.

May the Holy Spirit stir a hunger in you to see the captives set free through your life. Get ready for a life-changing encounter with the Lord as you read these pages with an open and humble heart.

—Michael Lombardo
Revivalist
Author of *Immersed in His Glory*
Host, *Awaken Live*
Founder, Life Poured Out International
www.lifepouredoutintl.org

John Veal's book, *Supernaturally Delivered,* is one of the most uniquely written books on deliverance out there. With every page, he takes you on a journey into the various chapters of his crash course with the realm of darkness, which changed the trajectory of his life. This highly recommended book will provide you with practical and foundational truths acquired from his own encounters with the powers of hell in order to help reveal various facets of deliverance. *Supernaturally Delivered* is honestly one of those books you will not be able to put down once you start reading it. John's experiential journey, coupled with sound revelatory teaching, will release keys to go from being supernaturally bound to supernaturally delivered!

—NAIM COLLINS
President, Naim Collins Ministries
Author of *Realms of the Prophetic*
www.naimcollinsministries.com

We live in a day and time where many do not want to acknowledge spiritual warfare or recognize the need for deliverance ministry. In *Supernaturally Delivered,* Dr. John Veal has done an exceptional job explaining the reality of the spirit realm and how to effectively engage in deliverance and freedom. He not only clearly teaches that Christians can have a demon, but also how to receive complete freedom from demonic bondage. I greatly appreciate his stance on not conversing with demons and the power of prophecy in deliverance. As a prophetic deliverance minister myself, I know this message is a now word for the body of Christ. If you have a passion to pray for others or you are looking for answers on how to walk a life of freedom and victory, this book is for you. It is a scripturally solid, no nonsense message, full of great supernatural wisdom and authority. Thank you, Dr. Veal, for this vital ministry and message.

—REBECCA GREENWOOD
President and Co-Founder, Christian Harvest International
Author of *Glory Warfare, Breaking the Bonds of Evil, Let Our Children Go, Defeating Strongholds of the Mind,* and *Authority to Tread*

As the head of the International Society of Deliverance Ministers (ISDM), I have the privilege of knowing many of the top-notch deliverance ministers around the world. I don't know

John Veal personally, but I certainly plan to get to know him. He has made a great contribution to the ministry of deliverance. I truly believe he is plundering the enemy's house, and this book will help countless others do the same. *Supernaturally Delivered* is a great book and a valuable resource in the spiritual battle we all face. I highly recommend this easy-to-read and hard-to-put- down work. Be informed and be equipped! Don't ever allow a struggle to become a habit!

Blessings,
—Dr. William (Bill) Sudduth
President, International Society of Deliverance Ministers

DESTINY IMAGE BOOKS BY JOHN VEAL

Supernaturally Prophetic:
A Practical Guide for Prophets and Prophetic People

SUPERNATURALLY DELIVERED

A PRACTICAL GUIDE TO
DELIVERANCE & SPIRITUAL WARFARE

SUPERNATURALLY DELIVERED

JOHN VEAL

DEDICATION

First and foremost, I dedicate this and all books that I will ever write to my Lord and Savior, Jesus Christ. It was truly written for His honor and glory.

This work is also dedicated to my spiritual mother, Ruth Brown, who passed away on June 24th, 2016. I was in Chandler, Arizona on a ministerial assignment when I received a call saying that my spiritual mom had passed away. I was devastated! I somehow managed to fall asleep afterward, with my face damp from tears. Later that night, something amazing happened. I awoke to unseen oil being poured on my head and an invisible hand touching me on the side of my face. This has happened to me before and I knew that it was the Lord. Somehow, this occurrence was different. I felt another presence with Jesus. It was Mother Ruthie! Mind you, I didn't see her or Jesus, but I felt them. This had never happened before and trust me when I say I don't believe in ghosts or people coming back from the grave! Somehow, someway, God gave my spiritual mom the opportunity to give me a final goodbye before going to heaven.

In the past, whenever I've had a visitation from the Lord, I only felt His presence. I can't explain how I knew it was her, but I did (tears are welling up as I am writing this). Soon they were both gone and I drifted back to sleep. The next morning, I ventured out. While in the midst of an arid day, I asked the Lord about what transpired the night before. He immediately responded with, "She gave you her mantle."

I hurried back to my hotel room and told my wife, Elisa, all that took place, even God's response to my inquiry. She calmly replied that she had been praying ever since I'd left. During her time with the Lord, He showed her a vision of a huge, beautifully colored mantle, layered with gold and rare gems. God told my wife that this was Mother Ruthie's mantle. Further stating that it was too big for one person and was being divided up to be given to all her spiritual children (she had many!). This essentially confirmed my experience the night before and I've never been the same since.

Ruth Brown was the most powerfully anointed woman I've ever known, especially when it came to prayer, deliverance, and fasting. Mother Ruthie loved me and treated me like her own biological son. I've never known anyone like her before or since her passing. She was so selfless and consistently put the welfare of others before herself.

Ruth always made herself available for those who came to her for prayer or deliverance ministry. All of Mother's words of wisdom, correction, encouragement, and love still resonate in my spirit to this very day. Neither this book, nor any other one I'll write in the future, would exist if it wasn't for her.

I love and miss you, Mom!

ACKNOWLEDGMENTS

To my beautiful wife, *Elisa*: I thank God that He loaned you to me to be my lifelong companion in this journey called life. You are the strongest woman I've ever known. When you became my wife, it was the answer to a childhood dream. You make me want to be a better man, husband, and father. I loved you when I first saw you, though I had no true concept of what love really was. It grows more with each passing day, hour, minute, and second.

To my firstborn, *Jennifer*: You are incredible! One of the greatest days of my life was your birth. You were prophesied about before you were even conceived. Don't ever quit on your dreams. I love you, Jen-Jen!

To my middle child, *Jessica*: Your compassion for others never ceases to amaze me. It always brings a smile to my face and encouragement to my heart. Don't ever allow the world or people to change you. I love you, Tex-Mex!

To my youngest child, *Jayla*: You are so much like your father! Your sense of humor is contagious and uplifting. Never lose it, even when the trials of life try to steal it. I love you, Jay Bird!

To *Dr. Hakeem Collins*: My God! You are awesome, brother! I truly thank God for your friendship, support, wisdom, humor, and love. I'm not one who easily uses the word *covenant*, but it definitely applies to us.

To *Brad R. Herman*: Thanks so much for acquiring me as an author for Destiny Image! You have proven to be a great friend and brother in Christ. I really appreciate your advice, logic, candor, intellect, and passion for the people of God. It's more than a job with you; it's a ministry. The best is yet to come for you!

To *Larry Sparks*: Your support, advice, and encouragement have blessed me. You are a pioneer of the supernatural as it relates to the things of God. I love how you've included books like the one you're reading now in the Destiny Image catalogue. Thanks again for giving me a platform to reach the world with the messages the Lord has given me.

To *Jevon Oakman Bolden*: You are amazing! Thank you for assisting me with the flow, feel, and organization of this book. Your offline advice has been invaluable. I'm so blessed to know you! You are a phenomenal editor and person.

To *Destiny Image Publishers*: Thank you for your unwavering support, encouragement, and diligence in bringing this book to life. Special shout out to Tina Pugh, Meelika Marzarella, Kyle Loffelmacher, John Martin, Wil Brown, Eileen Rockwell, and the rest of the Destiny Image team. I truly love and appreciate my DI family!

I would like to also thank the following ministries and people for their support: my entire Enduring Faith Christian Center tribe (past, present, and future), Liberty Temple of Chicago, Bolingbrook and Waukegan, Crusaders Church, Destined to

Win Christian Center, Power and Authority Church, Jeffery and Rhonda Veal, Earl and Bertha Rowe, Alicia and Damon Johnson, Andrais and Kairi Thornton, Joseph and Sharon Rowe, Trey and Jasmine Fisher, Michael and Carmolita Hubbard, Lamar Baker, Helen S. Wells, D'anne Tombs-Shelton, Steve and Lauren Mann, Jeffery and Seena Veal, Sherman and Vicki White, Joseph and Valerie Crofton, Kelvin and Tonya Easter, Joshua Botello, Sharon Peters, Deon and Antoinette Hill, Ivory and Evelyn Hopkins, John Eckhardt, Monroe Mullins, Randy Horn, Walter V. Williams, Sheanon Mays, Shirene Anderson, Naim Collins, Steve Shultz, Luis Lopez Jr., Lorenzo Irving, Kathy DeGraw, Elaine Tavolacci, Michael Lombardo, Kynan T. Bridges, Becca Greenwood, William (Bill) Sudduth, Scott Wallis, Sue Branch, Yvonne Lovelady, Ebony Murrell, Bernadette Washington, and a host of others—far too many to name.

CONTENTS

FOREWORD

Supernaturally Delivered: A Practical Guide to Deliverance and Spiritual Warfare by John Veal is written from a biblically sound and practical, insightful perspective. He shares his journey on the amazing path to deliverance and spiritual warfare.

Many of the examples John uses in this book the readers will be able to relate to. They will see how his family, as well as John, were brought to the place of deliverance and a ministry that helps so many. Deliverance workers have a new tool to use within this book.

The reader of this book will find not only deliverance principles, but an insight on spiritual warfare based upon firsthand experience.

It will not take the reader long to realize that John's life growing up was a deliverance work in the making. The enemy of our soul is really good at one thing—recognizing anointed vessels and families long before they are aware of it.

Supernatural deliverance is God's divine hand throughout this man of God's life. From the spirit of rejection's attempt to curse him at birth, to his bold journey with occult spirits through Ouija boards and other manifestations he and his family experienced.

The testimonies you'll read in this book are phenomenal and amazing! They will be living witnesses of how the power of God delivered him and his wife from demonic attacks, through which they learned tactical warfare against the enemy.

In this book, you will find that the supernatural should be an expected way of life in the walk of believers, not a surprising shock one stumbles into.

I believe that you will find your place, power, and prophetic destiny clearly explained in John Veal's book, *Supernaturally Delivered*.

It gives me joy to write the foreword for this book because in it I see what's dear to my heart: "Balanced Deliverance." This is biblical teaching about how the Lord delivers people according to His Word. It's when you see and hear more about the Word of God and the Holy Spirit than demonic manifestations.

This book is an excellent tool for the local church and Christian counselors. It will safely bring healing, insight, and deliverance.

Well done, soldier!

—Apostle Dr. Ivory Hopkins
General of Deliverance
Overseer and Founder, Pilgrims Ministry of Deliverance
Georgetown, Delaware
Author of *Deliverance and the Prophetic, Spiritual Warfare Training Manual Revisited,* and *Deliverance Guide to Marriage and Relationships*

INTRODUCTION

SUPERNATURAL DELIVERANCE IS YOURS!

Great deliverance giveth he to his king;
and sheweth mercy to his anointed, to
David, and to his seed for evermore.
—Psalm 18:50

When this book began to formulate in my spirit, musings about what it would contain consumed me. Basically, I wanted to use the spiritual occurrences within my own life to help illuminate various facets of deliverance ministry to the reader. The totality of these events sheds light on my attraction to the spiritual realm and, ultimately, its draw to me. I've always felt an intrinsic pull to goings-on in the spirit. My mother would periodically tell me, as I was growing up, that I was more spiritual than religious. I know this to be the truth.

In my first book, *Supernaturally Prophetic: A Practical Guide for Prophets and Prophetic People*, which I highly recommend getting (shameless plug), I share the culmination of my prophetic journey up to this point in my life.[1] This book, on the other hand, delves into the darker side of that same journey, chronicling how I was supernaturally delivered from evil powers.

As you get a bird's-eye view of the personal encounters that literally changed the course of my life, you may find their relevance to your own life. Accompanied by solid teaching, this book will help you to understand and apply the practice of supernatural deliverance so you too can be supernaturally delivered from everything that seeks to oppress, depress, bind, or entrap you. Along with real-world examples, useful application to biblical foundational truths will be provided.

EVERYDAY SUPERNATURAL

The supernatural ("departing from what is usual or normal especially so as to appear to transcend the laws of nature"[2]) should be a natural part of every believer's daily walk. It should be natural for us to negotiate the supernatural realm. It ought to be an everyday occurrence that we pray for people to be healed and they are, that we ask for wisdom and we get it, and that we tell the devil to flee and he does. We should be able to pray to God for angels to come and assist us here on earth and see it happen.

Each day, we should expect to see the mighty hand of the Lord moving in our lives and in the lives of those we impact. Our own lives should be evidence for the indwelling Spirit of God through divine expressions of kindness, compassion, gentleness, and self-control, as well as miracles, signs, and wonders. The Lord has mandated that we are to walk according to the Spirit and not after the flesh.

When Jesus was tempted by the devil, Scripture tells us that He was led by the Spirit (God) not the flesh. (See Matthew 4:1.) Now and then, the Lord will lead us into dark places in order to bring others out, which is the primary function of biblical deliverance or the casting out of devils. We may not comprehend why we face difficult seasons in our lives, but the answers make their appearance over time, possibly long after the ordeal has taken place.

Experience plus wisdom gained through maturity will cause us to know why we occasionally go through trying times. These encounters don't necessarily feel good, but there is an overcoming spirit attached to even the most terrible of testimonies when we come through them victoriously. Again, the Lord will allow you to go through them and come out on the other side stronger than when you went in, so that you can successfully pull others out of their troubles.

Often, the best person to minister to someone who's afflicted is one who's been delivered of a similar or identical affliction. This is one of my major reasons for writing this book. I'm going to be very transparent pertaining to what I've been through to further illuminate instruction that is solely based upon scriptural underpinnings.

The supernatural events that abruptly altered the course of my life may be a bit terrifying to some, so I'm giving you fair warning. If you are of a sensitive nature, you may want to stop reading here. But, if you're a child of God, there should be an absence of fear and an understanding that you have the power and authority to rebuke the spirit of fear (see 2 Tim. 1:7). If you know and believe that, let's continue.

ENCOUNTERS OF THE UNEXPLAINABLE KIND

For as long as I can remember, unexplainable manifestations have always played an important part in my life. I believe lots of followers of Christ Jesus can say the same thing. I've seen what some would call *ghosts* (a.k.a. demons in disguise). I've been attacked by unseen entities to the point that their violence left bruises on my body. While sleeping, I've been sat on by malevolent beings, unable to move. Some would call this sleep paralysis (a feeling of being unable to move). Disembodied, evil spirits have even spoken directly to me. I could go on and on about these and other demonic attacks, but I'll save them for you to catch up within the pages of this book.

When I first got saved, I just knew I was called to be a deliverance minister (a person who casts out demons). No one could tell me otherwise! I literally devoured any reading material I could get my hands on that dealt with deliverance. I was inextricably drawn to spiritual warfare (the ongoing battle between good and evil in the spirit realm: God and Satan), but I had no idea about how to war in the spirit. It got so bad and I had become so unbalanced that the Lord actually spoke to me saying, "That's enough. Focus on Me!"

Please understand: God wasn't rebuking me for learning about casting out devils. To the contrary, He was just letting me know that my emphasis was more on demons than Jesus Christ. You know what? In retrospect, He was right! Let me rephrase that: He's always right!

Proverbs 11:1 tells us that "a false balance is an abomination to the Lord: but a just weight is his delight." In everything that we do for the kingdom, balance must always be part of it. If it's unbalanced, then it's not kingdom! General of deliverance, Apostle Ivory Hopkins, makes reference to balanced deliverance in his book *Spiritual Warfare Training Manual Revisited*, which I highly recommend.[3] He writes about the importance of maintaining equilibrium in relation to practicing deliverance. There are many churches that ignore basic and practical deliverance even though casting out devils was the first thing Jesus said would be a sign of those who believe.

How can we neglect such a critical ministry? We ignore it to our detriment. Supernatural deliverance is integral to the life of every believer in Jesus Christ. It truly is the children's bread. (See Matthew 15:22-28.)

They Shall Cast Out Devils

And these signs shall follow them that believe; In my name shall they cast out devils; they shall speak with new tongues (Mark 16:17).

Many people today are oppressed and suppressed by Satan's emissaries of evil. They have an enormous longing to be supernaturally delivered, which can be achieved through total reliance on the power of God, in consonance (agreement) with the matchless name of Jesus Christ.

When we were instructed to perform deliverance on others, Jehovah commanded that we have authority over demons in His name. In the above Bible verse, the Lord says, "In my name shall *they* cast out devils." The responsibility falls upon us, not God. He's given Christians the authority in Yeshua's name to do it ourselves.

So why are there so many who are still bound by the enemy? The Lord uses individuals to facilitate His brand of deliverance, which may look a bit different from the processes witnessed today.

The Lord's brand of deliverance is effective deliverance. Simply meaning that when Jesus commanded evil spirits to leave a person, they did just that! Today, many struggle when attempting to cast out devils, often resulting in countless failed deliverance sessions. For example, there was an instance where several male ministers attempted to deliver a woman from multiple devils that had made their home in her body. During the deliverance, one of the demons spoke through the woman, addressing one of men of God, saying, "I'm surprised to see you here." The devil was insinuating that it knew or had previously *seen* the secret sin in his life. The minister, visibly shaken, left and never returned.

If you, as a deliverance worker, have unconfessed or unrepented sin in your life, evil spirits will perceive it. If you have demons, how can you cast out demons in others? As Jesus said in Matthew 12:25-28:

> *Every kingdom divided against itself is brought to desolation; and every city or house divided against itself shall not stand: and if Satan cast out Satan, he is divided against himself; how shall then his kingdom stand? And if I by Beelzebub cast out devils, by whom do your children cast them out? Therefore, they shall be your judges. But if I cast out devils by the Spirit of God, then the kingdom of God is come unto you.*

If Satan casts out Satan, then his kingdom would be in ruins. This course of action is counterproductive. It's my strong opinion that devils in the victim can join forces with the evil spirits in a demon-filled deliverance worker resulting in an ineffective and self-defeating session. It is God's will that ministers of deliverance be effective, but if they themselves are infected by devils, the result is oftentimes the opposite the Lord's will (freedom from enslavement to Satan). Unfortunately, people in need of major deliverance will suffer needlessly at the hand of an ill-prepared deliverance minister due to the lifestyle, character, and holiness of the facilitator.

The good news is that there is freedom for all. Deliverance workers who make it their priority to stay free from demonic infection can be used mightily by God. There's no getting around it: when the Lord wants to set people free from demonic oppression or possession in the earth realm, He will use His children to liberate those in bondage.

John 8:36 says, "If the Son therefore shall make you free, ye shall be free indeed." When Jesus sets you free, you're free! Once you obtain your release, it's your obligation to liberate others. This type of deliverance is meant to be permanent, unless we continue to open doors the Lord meant to remain shut.

LOVE MORE, FEAR LESS

In my life of strange and demonic encounters, I've had every reason to be afraid, but fear was really not a factor for me, especially after I made Jesus Christ the Lord of my life. Even after hearing the most inhuman voices come out of people while devils were cast out of them, there was this unusual absence of fear in my spirit, which surprised me at times. I'm telling you, once you've heard the ghastly voice of a devil, you'll never forget it! It's otherworldly, foreign to anything you've ever heard in this realm. I should have been afraid, but I have a better understanding now of why I wasn't. God has filled my heart with His love for people and especially those who are bound by the devil. Love is the very foundation of deliverance and spiritual warfare.

First John 4:18 says, "There is no fear in love; but perfect love casteth out fear: because fear hath torment." First John 4:8 tells us that God is love. When God (love) is on the inside of you, fear becomes foreign to you.

My spiritual mother, Ruth Brown, used to say that the closer you are to God, the more loving you should become—and I'll add to that: the more loving you become, the less control fear will have over you. Since I've come into a clearer understanding of the power love has in a believer's life, I've used Mother Ruthie's statement as a litmus test of sorts when others broadcast how much they pray or brag about their closeness to God. If there is no love in them as demonstrated by their actions toward others and their level of courage in the face of life's difficulties, then I have a hard time being convinced of their close relationship with God.

The following bears repeating: you may find some parts of this book disturbing. I only use these supernatural encounters to help illustrate how you can get through the darkness that tries to invade and overwhelm your own life.

It's my aim to inspire you to gain access to and maintain your own supernatural deliverance. I want you to be able to assist others in getting supernaturally delivered as well. This is God's desire for you too.

As we set out on this quest for supernatural deliverance, this is my prayer for you:

In the name of our Lord Jesus Christ, I pray that the person who is reading this book right now will begin to walk in supernatural deliverance as never before! I believe that they picked up this book because they desire to renounce every affiliation with every demonic entity that has gained entry. Therefore, I join with them and come against every generational curse that has attempted to permanently infect their bloodline. I ask that the curse be broken and that any attempt made by the enemy to affect their lineage be thwarted. I thank You, Father, that they will rejoice in the new liberty that You've afforded them through Your Son, Jesus Christ.

I pray that their gift of discernment be sharpened so that they can identify demonic infiltration before it begins. I pray that their eyes become like the eagle's so that they have the ability to see in the spirit and in the natural like never before.

Lord, let nothing come upon them unawares. Please cause them to comprehend exactly what they are seeing and download to them strategies to overcome the hordes of hell sent against them.

I come against poor spiritual vision, blurred eyesight, and blindness. I come against dullness of spiritual hearing and fogginess. Spiritually altered realities, fantasy, improvidence, myopia, and shortsightedness will have no place in their life, in the name of Jesus.

I pray that they won't have to experience tediously long sessions of deliverance. Let them speak the word only with the type of faith that causes demons to flee out of their bodies and lives in the name of Jesus! Let the oil that rests upon this book rest upon them, leaving a residue of deliverance. Let them walk in supernatural deliverance and confidence as never before.

Now, Father God, as they begin to walk in a new level of freedom and deliverance, I pray that You would empower them to cast out devils and set other captives free.

I thank You, Lord, that a mantle of deliverance will rest on those who are reading this and are called as ministers. I pray that any deliverance mantles that have been dropped by those long gone will be picked up and used in this season. Confirm the call that You have over their lives in multiple ways. Give them mentors after Your own heart who will train them up in deliverance, so that they can lead others to be supernaturally delivered! Amen.

I believe that Jesus wants you to experience everything He died to give you, and this includes a life of peace, wholeness, and victory over sin and the enemy of your soul. I pray that your faith for this reality increases as you read this book, and you begin to see without a shadow of a doubt, that victory is your portion. If you're ready to learn how you too can be supernaturally delivered, then let's begin!

PART I

MY STORY

CHAPTER 1

SEEDS OF REJECTION

I proceeded forth and came from God;
neither came I of myself, but he sent me.
—JOHN 8:42

My beginnings on Chicago's South Side were humble, yet fraught with peril and rejection. My parents, who were not married at the time of my conception, dealt with many challenges commonly faced by the young and in love. My mother's name was Beverly, and upon my arrival into this world, doctors told her I wouldn't make it through the night, but God said otherwise.

Immense pressure was placed on my mother, a frightened twenty-year-old, to give me away to a family in need of a child. This idea was endorsed by my biological father and maternal grandmother. My mother acquiesced to their demands and, almost immediately after I was born, put me up for adoption with a Catholic convent for unwed pregnant young women, which also served as an orphanage. I was there for what probably seemed like an eternity to her, but I added up the time and found it to be only about six months.

My mother mercifully snatched me out of that place and raised me as a single mom until she married a man named Jeffrey Veal during my preteen years.

I didn't find out about my *almost* adoption until much later in life. My mom held on to this secret for almost forty years! I am truly grateful for her resolve to go against the man she loved and her own mother in order to keep me and raise me herself. It amazes me to this day and caused me to love her even more, if that were even possible. I told her on many occasions that if I'd known of her sacrifices, I would have been nicer to her as a teenager. I was extremely rebellious in every way! Back then, I thought that she didn't really love me for a multitude of reasons. Upon reflection, I know without a doubt that she did. She passed away suddenly on January 20, 2009. It was one of the worst days of my life. In reality, that entire year was filled with disappointment and anguish. God rest her soul. I miss her.

REJECTION AND THE BASTARD SPIRIT

I often wonder what my life would have been like if my mother hadn't listened to the Lord and her own heart and retrieved me from that orphanage. What type of man would I have become without my current family? Who would have been my adoptive family? I'll never know. What I do know is that the spirits of rejection and bastardization had attached themselves to me. They were the strongmen that allowed other demons to invade my flesh as I continued on in life. Am I knocking adoption? Quite the contrary. I was adopted by another man (Jeffrey Veal) when my mother got married. There is great honor reserved for those who are courageous enough to procure and love children who, through no fault of their own, are essentially given away. These kids may feel a sense of abandonment, but they're never abandoned by God. What looked like an accident to the parents was intentional on the part of our Lord. I know this because I was one of them.

Many who are born out of wedlock have a tougher time in life than those who are born to married parents. The revelation God has given me on this does not come from any secular or Christian book. It was born out of my own firsthand experience. I noticed that rejection and bastard spirits are attached to each other. Where there is one, the other is often present. As an infant in the orphanage, I'm sure the enemy planted seeds of rejection that persisted and grew within me for many years afterward. When the spirit of rejection came in, so did the bastard spirit.

Bastard is defined by the King James Online Dictionary as "a natural child; a child begotten and born out of wedlock; an illegitimate or spurious child. By the civil and canon laws, a bastard becomes a legitimate child, by the intermarriage of the parents, at any future time. But by the laws of this country, as by those of England, a child, to be legitimate, must at least be born after the lawful marriage."[1]

I was a bastard in the natural until my mother married. I was illegitimate in the eyes of the world before this marriage. It's my belief that illegitimacy is a spirit that must be cast out. This spirit abides within the bastard spirit. They are *married* to each other. To be illegitimate means that something or someone is not authorized by law, standards, or birth. It's as if they've entered the world through an illegal transaction, which can be described as being born of sex outside of the confines of matrimony (also known as fornication).

Did you know that in order to be legitimate and recognized as royalty in England you have to be born to married parents? If you are a bastard there, there's no way you can ever be part of the royal family.

Thank God that it's not that way in the kingdom of God! As long as you're in Him, you're royalty! I am in no way co-signing to having sex outside of marriage. According to Scripture, it's still a sin. I'm just illustrating the point that it doesn't have to stop you from becoming who God called you to be. God will forgive you of fornication and cleanse your heart when you confess to Him and repent (see 1 John 1:9).

MEANT TO BE

Ye do the deeds of your father. Then said they to him, We be not born of fornication; we have one Father, even God. Jesus said unto them, If God were your Father, ye would love me: for I proceeded forth and came from God; neither came I of myself, but he sent me (John 8:41-42).

Being born out of fornication creates many issues in life, but they are not insurmountable. Victory over them all results from a personal relationship with Jesus Christ. Please don't feel condemned if you were an "oops" baby (unplanned pregnancy) or born out of wedlock. In 2007, a man who claimed to be an apostle, visited our church at a time when a pregnant teenager had just become a part of our ministry. The man boldly proclaimed that the baby inside of her was never meant to be born. I corrected him, saying that the developing fetus wasn't necessarily in the parents' immediate plans, but it was in God's future ones! The baby wasn't on their agenda, but it definitely was on the Lord's! Regardless of the manner of your birth, the direction of your destiny in Him has already been cemented. Hallelujah!

If this is your story, then rejoice in the fact that the Lord orchestrated that you be here on earth at this very time, and at this precise moment. I hope I don't come off as being conceited by writing this, but the Most High has used me greatly over the years—someone who was produced by parents who never married. Again, if this is you, remember that even though your biological parents didn't expect you, the Lord did! You're here on purpose, for purpose!

REJECTION IS AN OPEN DOOR TO THE ENEMY

Reject as defined by the King James Online Dictionary means:

1. To throw away, as anything useless or vile

2. To cast off; to forsake (Jeremiah 7:29)

3. To refuse to receive; to slight; to despise[2]

The spirit of rejection was a huge part of my life, especially during my teenage years. I always felt as though I didn't fit in with family or friends. I thought I was useless, and I wrestled with very low self-esteem. It didn't help that those around me almost always accentuated my weaknesses atop my strengths. My confidence was at an all-time low. I now realize that this was mainly due to how rejection accompanying a bastardized spirit invaded and affected my body, mind, and spirit.

So many in the church today need deliverance from the spirit of rejection. This spirit has caused many to leave houses of worship prematurely and sometimes Christianity entirely. The spirit of rejection also has a neighbor called the spirit of offense. Where you find one, the other is always stationed nearby, ready to come through the door rejection leaves open for it. When one is cast out, the other tends to follow.

WATCH YOUR WORDS, GUARD YOUR HEART

We must understand that the more we feed these spirits, the longer they stay. For example, the more we utter phrases of rejection or offense such as, "You're stupid," "You'll never amount to anything," "You're ugly," and so on, the stronger they (rejection and offense) become in our lives. These ill-advised expressions will eventually morph into strongholds that are difficult to tear down. Naturally and spiritually, we become the manifestation of our greatest thoughts, especially when those same thoughts become words.

Before we speak them, words are created within the heart and mind. Our thought processes actually find their genesis within our blood-pumping organ.

For as he thinketh in his heart, so is he (Proverbs 23:7).

According to Matthew 15:19, evil thoughts emanate or proceed from the heart. This is one of the reasons that the Bible warns us to guard our hearts because everything we do flows from it (see Prov. 4:23, NIV). To combat demonic spirits, we must maintain the mindset of our Lord and Savior, Jesus Christ.

Did you know that many of the crazy thoughts we get from time to time are not our own? They originate from Satan. When they come, we instinctively accept them as our own and tend to reproduce them with our lips. Our mouths and mentality are meant to glorify Christ, not entertain the blasphemous thoughts of devils or repeat their words.

Remember, you will eventually do whatever you speak or think about the most if given adequate time, space, and opportunity.

That ye may with one mind and one mouth glorify God, even the Father of our Lord Jesus Christ (Romans 15:6).

Our thoughts and mouths should be focused on the glorification of the Father, not the slanderous mental assaults of the enemy. I recall hearing a well-known pastor address a situation, some years ago, in which a man came to him asking how he could get rid of the crazy thoughts that plagued him on a daily basis. The shepherd instinctively responded, "When you find out, let me know because I still have them!"

The enemy's primary battlefield is our minds. He realizes that if he can hold sway over our brains, then our bodies will follow. I routinely draw comparisons between this and the pimp-prostitute relationship. As the pimp gains access to the prostitute's mind, he or she uses enticing lies to gain mastery over it. Consequently, control is established, and her body is enslaved. At this point, there's almost nothing the woman wouldn't do for the one who prostitutes her. This includes selling her precious body and giving the pimp whom she *thinks* she loves the wages earned on her back.

This is what many people who actually call Satan their lord do. They work for devils through counterfeit demonic leaders who exude false love toward them, *secretly* setting them up for their final destruction in hell (see John 10:10). These unfortunate individuals give the enemy their all without realizing that it's a setup to procure their souls. Again, if the enemy can get and keep your mind, your body and soul will follow. In order to stay supernaturally delivered, it's crucial to unwaveringly maintain the mentality of Jesus Christ. That way, Lucifer cannot infiltrate or control it.

PRAY FOR THE GIFT OF DISCERNMENT

In frequent instances, being deceived by the powers of darkness is a slow and deliberate process. One eventually finds themselves in a precarious situation, not fully understanding just how they reached a point of such obvious deception. This is why the development of the gift of discernment (see 1 Cor. 12:10) is so badly needed in the body of Christ, but it's neglected due to a number of Christians being disproportionately consumed with the other eight gifts of the Spirit. The devil counts on us being "visually impaired" when it comes to spiritual discernment because he doesn't want people to ever see him coming.

Early in my life, I was able to perceive things in the spirit, but not totally comprehend them. In order to avoid demonic penetration, you must be able to discern (see) the enemy long before he gains access to your temple (body). For all intents and purposes, you're spotting potential issues before they can mature into demonic manifestations. This way you can be supernaturally delivered before actual deliverance is required. When praying, ask the Lord for the gift of discernment. People who have this gift are "able to see or understand the difference; to make distinction; as, to discern between good and evil, truth and falsehood."[3] Once received, use it so that it won't become dull from inactivity. The more I use discernment in my own life, my ability to frustrate the enemy's future onslaughts increases. It can be the same with you. What the Lord does for me, He can certainly do for you. He shows no partiality (see Acts 10:34). Ask the Lord to increase this precious ability called discernment that He's given us access to. That way, you'll be able to stop Satan before he gets started in your life.

CHAPTER 2

CHICAGO HORROR STORY

And when they say to you, "Inquire of
the mediums and the necromancers who
chirp and mutter," should not a people
inquire of their God? Should they inquire
of the dead on behalf of the living?
—Isaiah 8:19, ESV

"It said it loved me and that I
would be its bride in hell!"
—Helen Wells

It was a dark and gloomy night...

Isn't that how most scary stories begin? Well, mine is no exception. However, what began in horror ended in victory! Let me take you back a bit, to a time when I was about six years of age.

My mother and I lived with my grandparents in a modest house located on the South Side of Chicago. My grandfather, Dr. S. Wales Shockley, who raised me like his own son, was a former army captain, preacher, and dentist. My grandmother, Nettie

Mae Shockley, who showed me unconditional love, was a stay-at-home mom who raised two successful daughters—my mother, Beverly Veal, an attorney, and her sister, Helen Wells, a principal.

On that same dark and gloomy night, my mom and aunt were immersed in a game where they held hands, intentionally, over a triangular-shaped object that had what appeared to be a magnifying glass in the middle. This object, I later learned, is called a planchette. As they played, it was as if the planchette moved on its own volition, traversing a medium-sized board with the entire alphabet, numbers one through zero, symbols (the sun, moon, stars, and other things), and the words *yes, no, maybe, hello,* and *goodbye* printed on it. When my mother or aunt asked it questions, it would answer by moving to various numbers, symbols and/or letters, spelling out words or numerical terminologies. They were playing with a *Ouija board.*

Mind you, I never actually played this game and had no idea of the triangular device's (planchette's) true designation. I did, however, enjoy pretending it was a racing car and sliding it around on the kitchen table from time to time. On this night, though, I observed them as they took part in an activity that inadvertently opened a doorway to the supernatural.

A DEMONIC PROPHECY

My mother received the most attention from whatever it was that lived on the other side of this piece of morbidly decorated wood. Initially, the communication was civil and benign, but it abruptly evolved into heinous and malicious nonverbal conversations. The thing said its true name was "Pluto" and that it hated my mother.

It felt so much ill intent toward her that it venomously expelled a phrase that would alter her life for the next ten years.

Methodically using their hands as his instrument to slowly move to each letter, the demon spelled out an alarming sentence, *"You will be dead in the next ten years."* My mother was twenty-six years old at the time, which, according to this *demonic prophecy,* meant that she would exit the land of the living when she reached her thirty-sixth birthday.

For continuity's sake, let's jump ahead ten years. I was sixteen years of age, and we were no longer living with my grandparents. My mother, father, little brother, and a German shepherd occupied a modest home in the southern section of Chicago. My mother began speaking very negatively concerning the end and/or brevity of her life, saying things like, "When I'm gone..." "Take care of your little brother." "Life is short." Her way of speaking was not totally surprising because her thirty-sixth birthday was just days away.

The evening before her birthday, I petitioned the Lord as hard as I could, pleading with Him to let her live and not die, and He answered my prayer. My mother didn't die at thirty-six, thank God! She lived for another twenty-seven years. Sadly, my mom did pass away suddenly at the age of sixty-three. The devil said she would die at thirty-six, but she made her home in heaven at sixty-three, which interestingly is thirty-six in reverse. This fact both baffles and concerns me to this very day.

Let me take you back once again to my grandparents' house that fateful night my mother received those cursed words, so we can look at what happened to my Aunt Helen.

The Devil's Bride

The room was ominously dark with only the light of slowly melting candles, flickering against the walls. Both women sat at the kitchen table, fingers pressed cautiously on the planchette. This time, my aunt began asking it a series of questions, and just like with my mother, the answers were innocuous (harmless) at first. But this changed relatively quickly. The planchette started to shift to letters that spelled out very foul and perverse words. The thing behind the board was, as some would say, cursing like a sailor. All of a sudden, this monster began to communicate directly to my aunt Helen. It spelled out, "*I love you. You will be my bride in hell*!" The demon spoke other vulgar words far too disgusting to mention here.

As a direct result of my mother's and my aunt's experiences, the Ouija board was expeditiously evicted from my grandparent's home to its new and permanent dwelling place—the garbage can! I clearly recall my mother's unbridled enthusiasm as she threw it away, box and all. There was a positive shift that was felt in our home once the Ouija board was gone, but, regrettably, it didn't last; some spirits still remained. There's always a price paid when you open doors the Lord has forbidden you to open.

As the prophet Isaiah said in the Scripture at the beginning of this chapter, when we desire answers, we must inquire of the Lord, not the dead. Those who use Ouija boards are mostly looking for solutions to some type of problem from people who have passed away. We can see this illustrated in First Samuel 28:6-19, when Saul, the king of Israel at the time, made this same dreadful mistake.

DON'T CONSULT THE DEAD

In First Samuel 28:6, Saul had a problem and needed answers, but he was no longer on speaking terms with God. He initially asked the Lord for an answer, but the Father didn't respond. When the king didn't hear from God, he decided to address his queries to an alternative source, a necromancer, one who consults the dead. This is how lots of men and women of God end up getting involved with psychics, witches, warlocks, and Ouija boards.

After getting the witch of Endor to bring up Samuel, the first thing out of the prophet's mouth was, "Why did you disturb me (call me up)?" (see 1 Sam. 28:15).

Saul answered, "I'm in deep trouble," and went on to say, "The Philistines are at war with me, and God has left me and won't reply by prophets or dreams. So, I have called for you to tell me what to do" (see 1 Sam. 28:16).

The only thing that can come from necromancy is death. When you speak to the dead, especially on a consistent basis, it can cause death to become contagious! Scripture lets us know that the payment for sin is death (see Rom. 6:23). Keep in mind that consultation with the dead is sin. Therefore, death gains access through sin and spreads over time if there is no ceasing of the ill-advised activity. To protect us, the Father intentionally warns us not to consult with those in the hereafter. Consulting with devils results in:

A departure from the faith

> *Now the Spirit speaks expressly, that in the latter times some shall depart from the faith, listening to spirits of error and doctrines of demons* (1 Timothy 4:1, JUB).

Uncleanness

> *Turn not unto necromancers and unto soothsayers;*
> *seek not after them to make yourselves unclean: I am*
> *Jehovah your God* (Leviticus 19:31, Darby).

Death

> *Thus died Saul, for his unfaithfulness where-*
> *with he dealt unfaithfully against Yahweh, over the*
> *word of Yahweh, which he kept not, (and, also, in*
> *asking by necromancy when he desired to enquire)*
> (1 Chronicles 10:13, REB).

By seeking a medium to question the prophet, Saul departed from the faith, became unclean, and later died. Many Bible scholars contend that this was not actually Samuel who was conjured up by the witch of Endor, but a demon masquerading as the prophet. I disagree. It's my opinion that, in this case, the Father allowed Samuel's rest to be disrupted in order to give Saul a rebuke from the Lord. Am I condoning actively seeking the dead for advice? Absolutely not! When you do, you are literally and spiritually playing with fire, and quite possibly, you are going to get burned.

GO TO GOD HIMSELF

When people feel they're not getting solutions to their problems from God, there's a tendency to seek out ungodly resources. For example, if a person doesn't take time to listen for the Lord's voice during prayer, they might say He's not speaking to them. During one of my intimate times with God, He told me that it's His desire to speak to His children. He's talking to many of them, but they're not taking the time to listen.

Let me recommend this: if you pray for an hour daily, take part of that time, whether it be fifteen minutes or a half an hour, to simply be quiet and listen for the voice of the Lord. If you do this with fidelity, you will begin to hear His voice and eventually become very familiar with it. The more you grow accustomed to it, the harder it will be for the enemy to trick you into accepting his voice as the one true voice.

I've always said that if you've talked to someone on a daily or consistent basis, you won't have to say, "Who is this?" when they call. Why? Because you *know* their voice. This is accurate in reference to your relationship with the Father. You won't have to consult the Ouija, using it a mediator between you and the Most High. You'll be able to hear God for yourself.

The word *Ouija* means "yes."[1] According to the English-Japanese Dictionary, it also means "yes; all right; OK; okay."[2] According to Dictionary.com, the Ouija board is "a device consisting of a small board, or planchette, on legs that rests on a larger board marked with words, letters of the alphabet, etc., and that by moving over the larger board and touching the words, letters, etc., while the fingers of spiritualists, mediums, or others rest lightly upon it, is employed to answer questions, give messages, etc."[3]

Another source says that the Ouija board is "also known as a spirit board or talking board, is a flat board marked with the letters of the alphabet, the numbers 0–9, the words 'yes,' 'no,' 'hello' (occasionally), and 'goodbye,' along with various symbols and graphics."[4]

A company called Parker Brothers came out with "The Ouija Board" in 1966. They didn't actually create a "game"—and please realize that it's not a game. The Ouija board is a tool used for demonic entry that existed long before Parkers Brothers got a hold of it. According to an article on the CANA (Christian Answers for the New Age) website:

> It arose out of the Spiritualist movement of the 19th century, a movement which was quite active at the time. Spiritualism is a practice (and a denominational religion) that is based on belief in contacting the dead.... The name Ouija is a combination of the French and German words for "yes": Oui and Ja.... The Board's translated name, "yes, yes," is an ingenious and subtle way to invite spirit contact.[5]

An Abomination

When you involve yourself with a device that's purpose is to contact those who make their abode in the afterlife, you're opening yourself up to entities that crave your eventual downfall. Heaps of times, when these spiritual doors are opened, they are extremely hard to shut.

Though my mother and her sister had no idea that what they were involved in was sinful, I believe my family's involvement with this "witch board" caused some issues to linger for years, but I thank God for the blood of Jesus! It defends us from the residue of our past misdeeds that were born out of ignorance. Still, I want it to be clear once again, so there is no misunderstanding: the Bible warns us against necromancy—consulting or summoning the dead. It is an abomination to the Lord.

There shall not be found among you any one that maketh his son or his daughter to pass through the fire, or that useth divination, or an observer of times, or an enchanter, or a witch. Or a charmer, or a consulter with familiar spirits, or a wizard, or a necromancer.

For all that do these things are an abomination unto the Lord: and because of these abominations the Lord thy God doth drive them out from before thee (Deuteronomy 18:10-12, emphasis added).

In verse 10, it says, "...that maketh his son or his daughter to pass through the fire." This phrase alludes to the practice of sacrificing children to the false Canaanite god, Molech. The writers of Compellingtruth.org reported:

The first mention of Molech is in Leviticus 18:21 in which the Lord commanded, "You shall not give any of your children to offer them to Molech, and so profane the name of your God: I am the Lord." The worship of Molech clearly involved ritual child sacrifice, something God's people were not to practice. This act was punishable by death according to Leviticus 20:2 which states, "Any one of the people of Israel or of the strangers who sojourn in Israel who gives any of his children to Molech shall surely be put to death."[6]

A TWISTED, UNHOLY LIE

The 2016 remake of the movie, *Ghostbusters,* used the catchphrase, "I ain't afraid of no ghost!"[7] As a believer in Jesus Christ, you don't have to be afraid. There is no place in the holy Scriptures that even hints at the dead roaming the earth as disembodied spirits. This is an invention of Satan! He is notorious for using God's truth, which is His Word, to establish his lies. The devil did this in the third chapter of Genesis. After the Lord warned Adam and Eve not to eat of the Tree of the Knowledge of Good and Evil, the serpent arrived on the scene and convinced Eve to do it anyway. He twisted the Lord's holy truth in order to unwind his unholy lie.

John 10:10 tells us that the thief's (Satan) job is to steal, kill, and destroy. The devil's falsehoods were designed take from you, murder you, and ultimately annihilate you. He wants to utilize half-truths in an attempt to extract the will of God from your life. He can't do this without your permission or agreement. The will of the Lord is always there, but Satan wants to keep you blind to it. How does he do this? Simply by persuading you to buy into his mendacities (lies).

> *Now the serpent was more subtil than any beast of the field which the Lord God had made. And he said unto the woman, Yea, hath God said, Ye shall not eat of every tree of the garden?*
>
> *And the woman said unto the serpent, we may eat of the fruit of the trees of the garden: but of the fruit of the tree which is in the midst of the garden, God hath said, Ye shall not eat of it, neither shall ye touch it, lest ye die.*
>
> *And the serpent said unto the woman, Ye shall not surely die: for God doth know that in the day ye eat thereof, then your eyes shall be opened, and ye shall be as gods, knowing good and evil.*

And when the woman saw that the tree was good for food, and that it was pleasant to the eyes, and a tree to be desired to make one wise, she took of the fruit thereof, and did eat, and gave also unto her husband with her; and he did eat. And the eyes of them both were opened, and they knew that they were naked; and they sewed fig leaves together, and made themselves aprons (Genesis 3:1-7).

The word *subtil* in verse 1 above means "sly, artful; cunning; crafty; insinuating."[8] The serpent was all this and more! He tricked Eve by using persuasive and deceptive language to latch on to what was already in her heart. The enemy will always attempt to entice us to do what's most evident in our hearts. He also will play upon what we think about the most. I heard a preacher once say that we become our greatest thoughts. As mentioned earlier, what we think on the most we will become or do.

Forbidden Fruit

We don't know how long she and Adam were in the Garden of Eden, but I imagine eating forbidden fruit crossed Eve's mind more than a few times. I'm sure Adam thought of doing it as well. This is evident by his lack of restraint when he ate the fruit his wife presented to him in Genesis 1:6. Sometimes the very thing we are told not to do becomes what we want to do the most. Proverbs 9:17 says that "stolen water is refreshing; food eaten in secret tastes the best" (NLT).

When we partake in ingesting forbidden fruit, it may be tasty at first, but the aftertaste is detrimental to our spiritual and natural health. At least, this was the case for Adam and Eve. They did something the Lord didn't approve of, and they lost their divinely privileged position in Him. Adam and Eve were subsequently banished from their beautiful garden, where life was apparently fancy, fun, and carefree. They found themselves in a place that was outside of paradise due to being deceived by Satan.

As previously mentioned, the devil's primary mission is to get you out of the will of the Lord. He will use what appears to be harmless to lure you into his domain. Satan is very patient when it comes to pulling you in. He'll meticulously plant seeds in you for years. Those same seeds will eventually germinate into maturity if they're continuously watered. You water them by consistently engaging in actions that please Lucifer. Next thing you know, you'll end up doing something that you swore you'd never do. Afterward, you wonder how you got into that adverse situation in the first place.

The devil can't make you do anything. The only power he has over us is the power we give him. I vehemently urge you to stay away from anything that deals with the occult (Ouija boards, tarot cards, séances, and the like). These practices and rituals can open demonic doors that may be extraordinarily hard to shut. Avoidance of such spiritually unauthorized pursuits will help to keep you supernaturally delivered. If you have any ties to the occult, renounce them now, in the mighty name of Jesus Christ. He can and will set you free from all demonic attachments, especially those that originated from ignorance. Do you want to be supernaturally delivered? Please repeat the prayer below:

Father God,
I come to You, humbly, asking for forgiveness for previous or current attachments to items or people involved

in occultic practice. I renounce every affiliation and participation, knowingly or unknowingly, with witches, warlocks, wizards, necromancers, voodoo, masonry, magic, new age, astrology, astral projection, divination, fortune telling, palmistry, automatic writing, vampirism, tarot cards, Ouija boards (please include any others you feel led to renounce here) and the demons within and behind them. I cut off all demonic cords that may have been hooked to me due to misadventure into forbidden realms of darkness. Lord, cleanse me of any satanic residue that remains that was tainted by demonic influences. Allow me to walk in the liberty that is You, which I haven't experienced in years! Father, I feel the devil's hold over me breaking! I sense a refreshing in the spirit coming over me now! Your love is renewing and filling every broken and infiltrated area of my soul. I thank You for forgiving me and I'm prepared to go forward in You, in Jesus's name! Hallelujah! (Praise Him now for His forgiveness and your freedom!)

TESTIMONY OF DELIVERANCE FROM A OUIJA BOARD

When I was first saved, the Lord reminded me that I had a Ouija board in my home. I was instructed to destroy it by fire.

When I walked into the room where this board was kept, I could not enter into the room even though the door to the room was open. It was like something out of a *Star Trek* movie! An invisible barrier was in that open doorway, and I would hit something I could not see each time I attempted to go into the room for it.

I called a couple of my Christian neighbors to come over, and we all prayed together, binding the spirit that would not allow me into the room. Finally, I was able to enter into the room and gather the Ouija board. We took it outside to set it on fire in the grill. As it was thrown into the fire, you could hear the screams of the demons attached to it as it burned.

This is one wicked game! It should be destroyed completely.

Afterward, I renounced the use of it. I repented for my ignorance in having and using it. From that point on, I was freed! —Name withheld[9]

CHAPTER 3

THERE'S SOMETHING IN MY HOUSE!

But when the priest comes and examines it, if the contamination has not spread in the house after it was replastered, he is to pronounce the house clean because the contamination has disappeared.
—LEVITICUS 14:48, CSB

My grandmother, mother, and aunt often spoke about our house being haunted. I was initially very skeptical, but a series of ominous, unexplainable events convinced me otherwise. These ghostly manifestations occurred before, during, and especially after the expulsion of the Ouija board.

My first encounter with the supernatural happened when I was about eight years of age. I was playing on the back porch of my grandmother's home and had to use the bathroom, so I ventured through the lowly lit kitchen to the restroom. I went in and instinctively closed the door behind me. As I reached up to turn on the light switch, I noticed a figure, which was darker than the darkness of the room and towering over me. The moonlight that peered in through the glass-block window provided me with its outline. Strangely, I felt very little fear—just awe and wonder.

The entity stood about six feet, a couple of feet taller than me at the time. I couldn't tell if it was male or female. My initial notion was that it could be my aunt. This thought was quickly dashed when I reached out, endeavoring to touch the shadowy character, while simultaneously inquiring, "Helen?"

To my astonishment, my hand just passed through it! This is the exact moment when the spirit of fear leapt into my body. The apparition appeared to gaze down at me and slowly began to turn away from me, proceeding in the direction of the adjacent bathtub. Once reaching it, it abruptly disappeared.

I stood there for a few seconds, which felt like an eternity, until panic got the best of me. I bolted out of the room, frantically searching for the nearest family member. I found Helen and relayed my paranormal meeting to her, like water being hurriedly poured into a glass. After listening intently, she simply and calmly responded, "I've seen it too."

It's Not Who You Think It Is

Once again, I want to make it clear that ghosts are not the spirits of our dearly departed. They are actually demons in disguise! Some believe that the dead walk the earth, constantly looking for the eternal rest in God that always seems to evade them. Hebrews 9:27 says, "It is appointed unto men once to die, but after this the judgment." According to the holy Scriptures, there is no purgatory. It's either heaven or hell. Even in biblical times, the disciples of Christ referenced ghosts.

> *And in the fourth watch of the night Jesus went unto them, walking on the sea. And when the disciples saw him walking on the sea, they were troubled, saying, It is a spirit; and they cried out for fear. But straightway Jesus spake unto them, saying, Be of good cheer; it is I; be not afraid* (Matthew 14:25-27, emphasis added).

The word *spirit* used in the Scripture above is defined as "an apparition; a ghost."[1] Matthew 14:26 states, "When the disciples saw him walking on the water, they were terrified. In their fear, they cried out, 'It's a ghost!'" (NLT).

If you ever see a deceased loved one manifest in your presence, rebuke the *ghost* in Jesus's name! It's not your family member or friend, but a malevolent spirit disguised as them.

Many of these demons or spirits inhabited the dearly beloved long before they expired, absorbing many of their experiences and memories. When they materialize, they'll have the same recall as the departed relative or friend. That's one of the reasons the Bible calls them "familiar spirits." (See Leviticus 19:31; 20:6,27; Deuteronomy 18:11; First Samuel 28:3-9.) They become familiar with their host, due to *living* in them, and can regurgitate various aspects of their lives with you upon request.

First John 4:1 admonishes us to try or test the spirit to see if it's of God. If it is, it will confess that Jesus Christ has come in the flesh. If not, it won't. I realize that this particular verse makes reference to the false prophet. I believe that it can also apply to the various demonic spirits that appear as apparitions in an effort to deceive us.

HE WANTS YOUR SOUL

The devil will not stop trying to lure an individual, even to the point of imminent death. I recall an episode of the television series *The Twilight Zone* that I watched as a child.[2] In this installment, an old man and his dog died simultaneously. They instantaneously found themselves on a road in the midst of what appeared to be a rural countryside. As they journeyed on, they happened upon a slightly obese male, wearing a straw hat and overalls. He looked friendly enough, so the older gentlemen engaged him in conversation in relation to their current state. The stranger beckoned the old man to come into his home, which was positioned some distance behind the fence that he leaned upon. The dog stiffened in response to the offer and began to bark furiously in protest. The stranger advised the old man to leave the dog, stating that canines were not allowed in. He pressured the seasoned gentlemen to enter without his faithful companion, assuring him that he'd enjoy himself. The old man declined, saying that if heaven wasn't good enough for his dog, then it wasn't good enough for him either.

In a huff, he and his dog trekked further down that country road under the echo of the stranger's protests behind him. Later, they come across a handsome young man, dressed in faded jeans and plaid shirt, armed with an ingratiating demeanor. The old man told how the stranger up the road tried to entice him to come into his home, but without his trusted companion. The younger gentlemen, with a stark look upon his face, sincerely expressed that he was so glad the old man didn't get mixed up with him.

He solemnly explained to him that what the stranger was offering wasn't heaven, but hell! The new acquaintance went on to tell the old man of all the benefits and blessing that awaited he and his dog. All three, joyfully, entered into the glory of what seems to be heaven.

I used this example to illustrate how persistent the enemy can be when it comes to acquiring your soul. Being the coward that he is, he'll patiently wait until we're at our weakest state before launching a full-frontal attack. These assaults commonly occur when we're on our sickbeds or in the process of making our final transition (death).

CALL ON JESUS; HE WILL SAVE YOU

There once was an unsaved woman who was deeply involved in the occult. As she lay dying, she actually saw demons insidiously crawling around her bed in anticipation. She told the people who surrounded her deathbed that they were there waiting for her to die so they could drag her to hell! Just seconds before she passed, the woman screamed, with eyes bulging and full of panic exclaimed, *"Help me! I'm burning!"* Then she died, with her mouth gaping and a terrifyingly twisted expression on her face. Witnesses reported that the woman looked as if she saw Satan himself! Unfortunately, there are many more awfully similar *"final last words"* spoken by those who didn't know Jesus Christ as their Lord and Savior while alive.

An authentic affiliation with God is the key to being supernaturally delivered from the clutches of the enemy, even at the end of our lives. He's so merciful that at the conclusion of your life, you can still repent, call upon Him, and He will save you. Satan has deceived many into thinking that He won't, but he's a liar. Don't fall for his lies! If you don't know Jesus Christ as Lord and Savior, then you can't experience supernatural deliverance. It's imperative that you know Him and make absolutely sure He knows you too. That way, the Most High will fill your house (body), and where the Holy Spirit fills, evil spirits cannot occupy.

YOUR SEASON TO CLEAN HOUSE

The items you bring into your home should be holy. If you aren't careful and well-informed, you can unknowingly bring demons into your household. Let this be your season to clean house. Ask the Lord to show you everything in your residence that is not of Him. You must understand that evil spirits use cursed objects— idols, paintings, totems, statues, music CDs, movies, downloads, and the like—as entry points. Be extra diligent when bringing objects into your house from countries whose god is not your God. Anything of a demonic origin must be cast out of the home and destroyed. If not, the dwelling is laid open to demonic penetration.

As a teenager, I unintentionally brought all kinds of demonic items into my parents' house. As a result, there was an increase in nefarious supernatural phenomena. During that time, I got into a huge argument with my mother. Don't look at me like that! I'm sure some of you are quite familiar with the rebellious teenager stage. As a result of our disagreement, I went to spend the night with my aunt. When I returned, my mother relayed an unbelievable story to me about what transpired after I left.

She was in the basement watching television, and the door to it suddenly slammed violently! My mother was initially startled, but later gripped by immense anger as she went up the stairs to see who the culprit was. When my mother reached the top, to her surprise, no one was there. She went to her bedroom, only to find her husband and my younger brother fast asleep in the bed. My brother, Jeff, was around three years old at the time. There's no way that he could muster up the strength to slam the basement door with such force.

My mom ventured toward my bedroom. The door was shut. She cautiously opened it and felt as if someone or *something* was behind it. As she peered into the darkness, a disembodied voice ominously said, "Come in." With that, my mother speedily closed the door and backed away from my bedroom.

Hearing her startling account upon my return home, I warily entered my room, immediately aware that my dresser had been pushed closer to my door. This prevented it from being opened fully. I guardedly searched my room, looking for an intruder. Finding no one, my mind started to wrap itself around the notion that the perpetrator could possibly be otherworldly (demonic). This was an alarmingly frightening conclusion. I prayed, laid in my bed, and apprehensively fell into a restless sleep.

As I previously noted, due to bringing demonic items into my room, something devilish gained admittance. I'm also of the mindset that evil entities lived in my childhood home before I brought in the accursed materials. It was reported that the previous owners frequently argued and fought. This type of atmosphere is a breeding ground for satanic activity. These demons, the former and latter ones, linked up and became even stronger.

Please remember, demonic strength is nothing compared to the power of the Lord! Demons are only as powerful as we allow them to be in our lives. In this case, knowledge is power. When you acquire knowledge of them, you'll in turn discover how to defeat them and remove their influence in your home and in your life. Tormenting demons have no place in your life as you seek to live as one who's been supernaturally delivered.

PART II

"LET ME IN!" DEMONIC ENTRYWAYS

CHAPTER 4

PERMISSION GRANTED

Submit yourselves therefore to God. Resist the devil, and he will flee [run in terror] *from you.*
—JAMES 4:7

Incorporeal spirits or demons require our permission to dwell in us. They receive this authorization through omission or commission. *Omission* is defined as "someone or something that has been left out or excluded."[1] *Commission* is "an instruction, command, or duty given to a person or group of people."[2]

Evil spirits gain access to people's lives through ancestry, accident, or acceptance. They can enter by the directive or command of the individual (commission). It's the willful act of inviting demons into a person's body. Witches, warlocks, and other followers of Satan do this. Instead of a *duty* being given to people, as the definition implies, authorization or access is being allotted to devils. Willful sin can also be a door of invitation to demons. This provides the enemy an occasion or chance to enter you.

Don't give the Devil a chance (Ephesians 4:27, GNT).

When referring to omission, the demon can be allowed entry through tragic events of which the individual had no control, such as rape, molestation, child abuse, sexual assault, and similar kinds of trauma. I cited the previous examples because I've witnessed the victims requiring deliverance from spirits that gained admission as a result of these abuses inflicted upon them. The sufferer has no culpability in these situations, but the acts themselves have the potential to cause demonic impregnation. In the case of molestation, it's often said that victims of abuse have a proclivity to abuse others. This could be the result of demonic influence or inhabitation.

Demons can also enter through someone in the person's lineage who dedicated their future offspring to Satan. In other words, devils can be inherited. An example of this is cancer, which I believe is an evil spirit that originates from the satanic realm. This demon kills thousands of lives annually. According to the National Cancer Institute, in 2018, an estimated 1,735,350 new cases of cancer will be diagnosed in the United States and 609,640 people will die from the disease.[3] This insidious evil seems to manifest itself in and through families. You'll see it passed down from father to son and mother to daughter, in many cases regrettably. But the good news is that cancer, as a spirit, can be cast out. Hallelujah!

It also appears that devils are not only familiar but also familial, meaning that they are assigned to families. When a demonized relative dies, that same demon or demons will seek refuge in another "open" person within the same family. By open, I'm implying that the family member is receptive or accessible through a sinful or unsaved lifestyle. This leaves them vulnerable to demonic occupation. In this case, the infected person had nothing to do with the familial or familiar infection. As I previously addressed, someone in their lineage dedicated or offered them up to the devil. The only thing that can save them is a true relationship with Jesus Christ, accepting Him as their Lord and Savior. This is the only way they can begin the process of being supernaturally delivered.

The following bears repeating—sin opens the door to demonic infiltration. Satan just waits by the door until you give him an invitation to come inside. Like a mythical vampire that frequents horror movies, he's not allowed in until you let him in. This invite is sent out when we involve ourselves in activities that are outside the will of the Lord. When in the enemy's territory or his will, we are subject to invasion. The Lord will often warn us when we're venturing out of His jurisdiction.

There were two incidents that led me to believe that demons need permission to invade a person's life. The first occurred when I was a teenager. I was lying in my bed, and the room was empty. Just before falling asleep, I felt as if something else was in there with me. I began to feel this *thing* floating above me, attempting to pull my soul out of my body! It felt as if I had a choice to either give in to it or fight. I chose the latter. It's difficult to accurately describe how I knew at the time; I just did. Today, I would say it was divine discernment.

The second incident transpired when I was much older and living in my current home with my wife. Again, I was in bed, experiencing a twilight moment—the sensation of being awake and falling asleep at the same time. Within this moment, I heard a seductively wicked voice speaking to my spirit. I knew it wasn't the Lord. It asked me, *"Will you let me into your body?"*

"No!" I said repeatedly, adding the demon-busting name of Jesus Christ, until it was gone.

SUBMIT TO GOD AND RESIST THE DEVIL

It's my belief that if I had answered in the affirmative, I would've given the demon a *right of entry*. If you submit to the devil, you empower him to invade you and, consequently, wreak havoc in your life.

When it comes to revoking Satan's right of entry, your response to him must be resistance at all cost. If you resist him, then he will flee, which, as used in James 4:7, means "to flee, escape, shun, to run away; by implication, to shun; by analogy, to vanish."[4] A former pastor of mine used to say that flee used here meant to run in terror. I've always loved that and clung to his definition. There's nothing like experiencing the enemy of our souls running away in a panic! Many quote the second part of James 4:7 but neglect the first part: "*submit yourselves therefore to God.*" This is the most important part of the verse. We must first submit to the Lord before we can properly resist the devil. Without submission, there can be no divine resistance; at least this is so within the kingdom when dealing with the adversaries of the cross.

When you live a life of submission to the Most High, you perpetually walk in His authority. The more submitted to His will you are, the more terrified the devil becomes of you. Why? Because His will becomes your will. There is no place safer than being in the perfect will of the Lord. Satan somehow knows who belongs to the Lord and who doesn't. There is no fear factor involved when he attacks those who don't know the Lord.

CAST HIM OUT WHERE?

When you resist a devil, personally, or cast a devil out of someone else, where do they go? They go where you command them to go. Remember when Jesus cast out the multitude of devils in Mark 5:9? The demons implored Him to send them into a herd of pigs, and He did.

When deliverance is taking place, the demonic forces must be sent somewhere specifically. I was always taught by my spiritual mother, Ruth Brown, to send them to the pit. The verse below states where they go when they leave an individual.

> *When an evil spirit leaves a person, it goes into the desert, seeking rest but finding none. Then it says, "I will return to the person I came from." So it returns and finds its former home empty, swept, and in order. Then the spirit finds seven other spirits more evil than itself, and they all enter the person and live there. And so that person is worse off than before. That will be the experience of this evil generation* (Matthew 12:43-45, NLT).

OUT WITH THE EVIL, IN WITH THE HOLY

What's interesting about the Scripture above is that it begins with "When an evil spirit leaves a person." It's my estimation that there are times when some demons just leave without going through a deliverance session. This can happen when an infected person gets saved (Jesus becomes their Lord and Savior). For example, before salvation an individual may have smoked cigarettes. The desire for nicotine miraculously vanishes immediately after a true conversion! The spirit behind the addiction left due to the Holy Spirit coming in.

> *And now you Gentiles have also heard the truth, the Good News that God saves you. And when you believed in Christ, he identified you as his own by giving you the Holy Spirit, whom he promised long ago* (Ephesians 1:13, NLT).

Once we believe, we're given the Holy Spirit. Now there is a difference between receiving the Holy Ghost and the manifestation of the gifts of the Holy Spirit. The gifts come to the surface after being filled with the Holy Spirit.

STARVE THEM OUT

There are times when demons just leave when God comes in. They may also exit due to starvation. Demons fulfill their illicit desires through human beings. They are incorporate beings who require a body to express their perverseness. If a person overcomes alcoholism and totally abstains from drinking, then the demon behind it might automatically leave. Why? Because the person is no longer "feeding" it.

By feeding them, I'm referring to a person doing the act(s) that the demon(s) desire. Not providing nourishment to devils is similar to going on a God-directed fast (not eating). Jesus said in Mark 9:29, "This kind can come forth by nothing, but by prayer and fasting." The latter gives evidence to the starvation of an evil spirit. Demons will leave when they can no longer express themselves, eat, or quench their thirst.

The desert mentioned in Matthew 12:43 refers to an area of isolation and exhaustion. Rest is foreign or unobtainable here for demonic entities. The demon goes here to strategize, awaiting an opportunity to return.

My former pastor, Randy Horn, used to always say that the devil doesn't have any new tricks. He usually comes to you with what he had you bound with in the past. For instance, if alcohol was your vice, he's not going to come at you with women. The enemy will approach you by appealing to what you are craving the most.

We've looked at how the enemy gains entrance into our lives and briefly touched on how we can be proactive in denying him that access. In the next two chapters, we're going to look at some specific entryways he uses to get in.

CHAPTER 5

HERE TO DESTROY

*The thief's purpose is to steal and kill
and destroy. My purpose is to give
them a rich and satisfying life.*
—JOHN 10:10, NLT

My grandfather, Dr. S.W. Shockley, used to be a preacher. He didn't stay one due to personal reasons. Dr. Shockley was an officer in the United States Army, a college graduate, a retired dentist, and is currently listed in the *Who's Who Among Black Americans*. I only list his credentials to further validate what I'm about to tell you. Dr. Shockley led an extraordinary life that was full of unexplained, supernatural events.

My grandfather became very ill in his early seventies. In this particular instance, he'd lost an enormous amount of blood. He was taken to the hospital where he lay in bed, physically and spiritually fighting for his life. At his weakest point, according to him, an unseen force entered the room. He couldn't see it, but he could sense and hear it. Abruptly, the entity began to speak. It said, *"I'm not here to help you. I'm here to destroy you!"*

After uttering these foreboding words, the presence was gone, leaving him in a state of fear and bewilderment.

This incident is typical of demonic assault. These spirits often come when they think you're at your weakest. Satan, being the *namby-pamby* (spineless) spirit that he is, will launch his minions against you, believing that you're too infirmed to fight back. His goal is your total destruction.

> *The thief cometh not, but for to steal, and to kill, and to destroy: I am come that they might have life, and that they might have it more abundantly* (John 10:10).

Satan is the thief referred to in this verse. In the natural, there are thieves who steal, kill, and destroy. This is the enemy of our soul's aspiration. He exercises such deviant pleasures through people who expose themselves to his demonic realm. In the past, I've seen murderers on television who committed horrific and unspeakable crimes asked why they did it. Most responded with "I don't know" or "I can't recall."

I have confidence in the fact that, in certain cases, Lucifer blinded their minds before and during the act. His forces, stationed within the individual, took over or possessed them totally for that moment, committing the heinous crimes through them. He deliberately waited for an opportune moment. The devil strategized for years, then manifested his plan when wrath took over.

Anger is an entry point for the enemy, as well as jealousy, evil thoughts, going our own way, and pride. Let's look now at how the enemy uses these thoughts and emotions to try to steal, kill, and destroy the abundant life God has for us.

ANGER

Rage is a potential doorway for devils because it usually leads to sin. The enemy realizes this and uses it to his advantage in the ongoing war against the saints. This is why the Bible cautions us not to allow anger to cause us to sin in the sight of the Lord.

> *Be ye angry, and sin not: let not the sun go down upon your wrath* (Ephesians 4:26).

In most cases, wherever there is anger, sin is not far behind. It positions itself at the door to the Lord's temple (your body), waiting for you to open it. This was clearly a factor in the first murder in biblical history, as recorded in the Scripture below.

> *And in process of time it came to pass, that Cain brought of the fruit of the ground an offering unto the Lord. And Abel, he also brought of the firstlings of his flock and of the fat thereof. And the Lord had respect unto Abel and to his offering: but unto Cain and to his offering he had not respect. And Cain was very wroth, and his countenance fell.*
>
> *And the Lord said unto Cain, Why art thou wroth [angry]? and why is thy countenance fallen? If thou doest well, shalt thou not be accepted?* ***and if thou doest not well, sin lieth at the door.*** *And unto thee shall be his desire, and thou shalt rule over him* (Genesis 4:3-7, emphasis added).

In a moment of intense irritation, Cain killed his brother, Abel. I subscribe to the theory that it wouldn't have transpired if Cain didn't already have built-up resentment toward him.

JEALOUSY

Another aspect of Cain's story is how he was given over to demonic forces by way of the spirit of jealousy.

> *If thou* [Cain] *doest well, shalt thou not be accepted? and if thou doest not well, sin lieth at the door. And unto thee shall be his desire, and thou shalt rule over him* (Genesis 4:7).

In Genesis 4, Cain slew Abel out of a jealousy derived from his more excellent sacrifice (gift) to the Most High. Wherever there is envy or covetousness, Satan is present. The devil was indirectly involved in the murder of Abel, the first prophet during biblical times, according to Luke 11:50-51.

Jealousy is sin, and when sin is allowed to make its home within you, demons can become occupants as well. This is especially true when this spirit is allowed to live in you for a lengthier duration of time. The longer jealousy stays, the more likely further demonic intrusion.

> *Wherever there is jealousy and rivalry, there is disorder and every kind of evil* (James 3:16, GW).

From reading the verse above, we can infer that all kinds of evil are attached to the spirit of jealousy. Again, this caused Cain to commit the first murder recorded in Scripture. My point is that sin, or demons, lie in wait by the door, encouraging us to do that which is unseemly in order to gain entrance into us. It's my stance that the phrase "sin lieth at the door" referenced in Genesis 4:7, describes how it's always waiting for the chance to rule over us. We must be ever ready and diligent to make sure this doesn't happen.

EVIL THOUGHTS

Though Adam and Eve were cast out of the Garden of Eden and raised their family outside its boundaries, the snake didn't stop speaking to the "first family" after being revealed. The devil continued to talk and play upon their thoughts, feelings, and beliefs. He especially wreaked havoc with Cain's embittered feelings toward Abel, cultivating them like seeds and watering them with his words. Like speaking to plants provides them with much needed carbon dioxide, Satan's falsehoods nourished the negativity that was already lodged in Cain's heart.

The enemy planted the seeds, then patiently waited for them to sprout. Cain's murderous act was more than likely played out in his mind countless times before he ever committed it. I'm sure that even you have entertained actions, conceptually, that you've never actually carried out.

Evil thoughts don't always originate with you. They are often given to you—an unwanted gift from the kingdom of darkness. Instead of speaking such things into your mind, Lucifer has an intense conversation with your heart. Your heart, in response, relays that dialogue to your mind. The brain then transports those evil thoughts to your mouth. Your mouth, in turn, translates them into words and they begin to pour out. Once spoken, consistently, there is great potential for the wicked consideration or thought to be acted upon.

For out of the heart proceed evil thoughts, murders, adulteries, fornications, thefts, false witness, blasphemies (Matthew 15:19).

In the case of Judas Iscariot, the betrayer of Christ, the devil influenced him for some time. He didn't take full control of him until Jesus revealed in John 13 that there was a traitor amongst the twelve disciples. Once fully inside, he dictated Judas's actions through a domination of his soul, mind, and body. When Jesus told him to do what he was going to do quickly, He was actually speaking to Satan himself, not Judas.

And after the sop Satan entered into him. Then said Jesus unto him, That thou doest, do quickly (John 13:27).

GOING OUR OWN WAY

When Judas was exposed and made up his mind to betray Jesus, Satan entered him.

Then entered Satan into Judas surnamed Iscariot, being of the number of the twelve. And he went his way, and communed with the chief priests and captains, how he might betray him unto them. And they were glad, and covenanted to give him money. And he promised, and sought opportunity to betray him unto them in the absence of the multitude (Luke 22:3-6).

Notice that the above scripture says, "*He went his way.*" The act of going our own way instead of God's takes us out of His will, placing us in the will of the evil one. Once in the territory of

Lucifer, he gains access to our temples (bodies). In order to prevent this, we must ever be mindful to stay within the will of the Father and go the way that He directs us.

Pride and the Spirit of Celebrity

For by the grace given to me I say to every one of you not to think more highly of yourself than you ought to think, but to think with sober discernment, as God has distributed to each of you a measure of faith (Romans 12:3, NET).

The celebrity spirit I see within the body of Christ these days is disheartening. Men and woman are beginning to worship Christian leaders more than God. What's even more alarming is some leaders are allowing them to do so! This is dangerous within itself. God will have no other gods exalted above Himself (see Exod. 20:3). He will not give His glory to another (see Isa. 42:8).

Today, we have too many *little gods* acting as God. They prefer to be the receivers of the glory rather than reflectors of the glory, refusing to give God all the glory. Instead of serving, they demand to be served.

Pride is a result of believing all the hype that goes along with celebrity. In other words, you begin to believe your own press.

As God elevates an individual, his or her true nature is slowly revealed. If they're arrogant inside, it becomes apparent on the outside. Conceit and the pulpit should repel each other, not attract each other.

How can one be a man or woman of God and think like a celebrity? The celebrity mindset, in a worldly sense, is one of excess, selfishness, narcissism, and vain ambition. Its goal is self-elevation and prosperity. Essentially, it becomes all about the person, not the people they're supposed to serve. Jesus Christ never walked in such a manner or spirit!

This mindset will eventually cause one to fall from grace. The Lord will send warning before taking from them their *kingdom*—notoriety, platform, and money garnered through ungodly celebrity.

> *Pride goeth before destruction, and an haughty spirit before a fall* (Proverbs 16:18).

There is always a downside to walking in pride. Pride is a spirit that needs to be rebuked whenever it rears its ugly head. This spirit targets the heart and seeks entry into the spiritual chambers of it. We give pride accessibility when our exploits start to become more about us and less about Him.

To keep the spirit of pride at bay, always give God the praise for anything you do in regard to the kingdom. For example, when complemented for doing kingdom work, rather than replying, "Thank you," saying, "Praise God, thank you," instead. Always give Him the glory first!

Pride has caused the downfall of many a great leader. Don't let the same thing happen to you! Remember, pride caused the fall of Lucifer, who later became known as the devil.

> *How art thou fallen from heaven, O Lucifer, son of the morning! how art thou cut down to the ground, which didst weaken the nations!*
>
> *For thou hast said in thine heart, I will ascend into heaven, I will exalt my throne above the stars of God:*

I will sit also upon the mount of the congregation, in the sides of the north: I will ascend above the heights of the clouds; I will be like the most High.

Yet thou shalt be brought down to hell, to the sides of the pit (Isaiah 14:12-15).

No matter how high the Lord takes you, stay humble. You'll be challenged not to be and sometimes you may slip, but continued practice will cause humility to cement within your spiritual DNA. As soon as you recognize pride swelling up in you, rebuke it, repent for it, and allow the Lord to reset you. If you do this, the swelling will go down. We all can get caught up in this spirit; no one is exempt.

According to First Samuel 15:17, Saul was little in his own eyes (humble). This, according to the prophet Samuel, caused the Lord to anoint him as the king over Israel. After he became king, humility was evicted by pride from his temple (his body). Mind you, it wasn't an immediate eviction, but the belongings of humility were moved out over a period of time. I've seen this happen in numerous peoples' lives. They start off right, but end up wrong, due to arrogance moving in and kicking out humility!

In order to be supernaturally delivered from the celebrity spirit, you have to consistently walk in humility. Make it a lifestyle. Practice makes perfect!

KEYS TO STAYING HUMBLE

1. Remember who you were before God delivered you.

2. Maintain a consistent prayer life.

3. Always defer or deflect the praises of people to God.

4. Don't believe the hype!

5. Recognize when you act arrogantly.

6. Participate in self-deliverance as needed.

7. Don't ever think you're incapable of falling.

8. Remember, the greatest chance of falling is right after a major victory.

9. Be quick to apologize, even when you're not wrong.

10. Bless the Sauls (persons who misuse their authority over you or are jealous of you) in your life.

11. Submit to godly authority.

12. Let go or get delivered from the spirits of rejection and bitterness.

13. Make up your mind to be an enthusiastic worshiper of the Lord!

14. Don't let the enemy consistently whisper in your ear.

DON'T LET HIM DRIVE

If you allow the devil to ride, he's eventually going to want to drive. Like he did with Judas, Cain, and King Saul, the enemy will spend years working on an individual. By the time they realize it, he's already taken over a great portion of their will. This is the primary reason why some people can't give up habitual sin (i.e. masturbation, pornography, fornication, homosexuality, etc.). If the devil inside wants whatever it is, it will use the human body to quench its demonic lusts. That's why a lot of Christians struggle with sins that they hate. It tends to cause shame, embarrassment, and anger. This is all an elaborate plan by the prince of darkness to cause your destruction. *Don't ever allow a struggle to become a habit!* A struggle is when you fight against sinning, but are often unsuccessful. A habit is when you willfully sin, without any thought or conviction about how it hurts God.

Everything the devil gives you comes along with a *demonic disclaimer*. A disclaimer is defined as "a statement that denies something, especially responsibility."[1] Lucifer will get a person to commit a crime, then abdicate his responsibility for it. He'll abandon the individual in the midst of the consequences of the act. Basically, they're left to take the rap for what Satan did through them. This is the epitome of his cowardice; however, this is his nature. He throws rocks, then hides his hands.

Be careful not to entertain a voice that seeks your elimination, not your elevation. Just like we must know the voice of the Great Shepherd (God), we must also know the voice of the stranger (Satan). By recognizing both voices, we're better able to discriminate between the two. One's aspiration is to assist you, while the other's aim is to harm you. When you are able to differentiate between the two, you're more likely to maintain your supernatural deliverance.

CHAPTER 6

UNCLEAN SPIRITS AND CURSED OBJECTS:
BOOKS

After throwing him into convulsions,
*the **unclean spirit** cried out with a*
loud voice and came out of him.
—MARK 1:26, NET, emphasis added

Did you know that demons have a stench to them? Their vomit-inducing odor can sometimes be perceived in the spirit, but there can also be a manifestation of it in the natural. Throughout the Bible, evil spirits that possessed men were referred to as "unclean spirits" as evidenced in the following verses:

> *And there was in their synagogue a man with an unclean spirit; and he cried out* (Mark 1:23).
>
> *And when he was come out of the ship, immediately there met him out of the tombs a man with an unclean spirit* (Mark 5:2).

And as he was yet a coming, the devil threw him down, and tare him. And Jesus rebuked the unclean spirit, and healed the child, and delivered him again to his father (Luke 9:42).

Unclean, as defined by the KJV Bible Dictionary, means "not clean; foul; dirty; filthy."[1] *Foul* is defined as "offensive to the senses, especially through having a disgusting smell or taste or being unpleasantly soiled" ("a foul odor").[2] There are countless reports of fetid smells accompanying demonic activity. I can attest to this fact, because I experienced their odor firsthand. It's like no other putrid smell that you've been subjected to on earth!

My experience occurred when I was a rebellious teenager with a gift I didn't fully comprehend (to hear more about my "gift" get my book, *Supernaturally Prophetic: A Guide for Prophets and Prophetic People*, available at bookstores nationwide). At the time, I lived with my mother, father, little brother, and our dog in a modest, middle-class home on the south side of Chicago.

Because I couldn't explain my supernatural abilities—or myself—I started exploring books on the occult not realizing the peril of my actions. I devoured books on subjects that dealt with ESP (extra-sensory perception), clairvoyance, psychic readings, horoscopes, and the like. I actually stole these books from my school library. Keep in mind I was sixteen years of age, undelivered and unsaved.

I don't recall the titles of all the material I read, but suffice it to say, they were writings that opened up doors that should have remained closed. These books included the names of demons and various incantations (spells). Ignorantly, I brought these books home and stored them in the closet of my bedroom. Little did I know that, by doing this, I inadvertently brought "monsters" into our house and strange things began to occur almost immediately. The events that took place still bring a chill to my spine almost every time I recall them.

CLOSE THE BOOK, CLOSE THE DOOR

The first thing I noticed was my closet, where I kept the books, was always cold. My bedroom would consistently be toasty warm in the winter, yet where I hung my clothes would be freezing! I realized, later in life, that coldness within a space that has no natural origin can emanate from an evil source. There was also a very demonic feel to my sleeping area. I would attempt to get the family pet to stay in my room, but he would circle, whine, and scratch my closed door, eager to get out! To the best of my recollection, I don't think my dog ever voluntarily came into my room. Animals have a tendency to see, hear, and sense things in the spirit realm that we sometimes cannot.

When you have a call upon your life, the devil wastes no time leading you in the wrong direction when you're not purposely submitted to God. My rebellion and curiosity caused me to inadvertently venture into territory that belonged to Satan. When I look back, I can see that the spirit of anger weighed heavily upon me. It had even taken up residence within my parents' home, mainly in my room.

Years later, a minister and friend of mine at college gave me a word of knowledge (prophetic words that relate to your past or present) about books being in my closet that were portals for devils. He'd seen it in a vision and warned me to get rid of the books as soon as possible. I followed his instructions and did just that when

I returned home for break. When it was done, things got a bit better. I realize now that the iciness in my closet was caused partially by doors that were opened when I brought these occultic books home. In getting rid of them, I closed the book on that chapter of my life. I also shut one of the gates that gave the enemy admission into my life.

EACH BOOK HAS ITS OWN SPIRIT

Beloved, do not believe every spirit, but test the spirits to see whether they are from God, for many false prophets have gone out into the world (1 John 4:1, ESV).

Throughout my experiences, like the one shared above, I have discovered that books and other objects that we innocently bring into our homes can have spirits attached to them. If these spirits are evil, they can bring on satanic attack. Books were the main type of cursed object I personally held on to. You may have other items you've collected that need to be removed from your home and destroyed. There shouldn't be anything that separates us from experiencing the full blessing of liberty in Christ. He paid too high a price for our freedom for us to hold on to things that enslave us. This is especially true when we have rights through the blood of Jesus, to rule and reign in the kingdom of light.

Some have a tendency to believe that books are harmless. As a result of my experience, I want to share what the Lord has taught me in this area.

A Demon-Impregnated Paperback

During a conversation with my late spiritual mother, the awesomely anointed author, prophet, and prayer warrior, Ruth Brown,

I told her of a strange occurrence involving a paperback that I was currently reading. It was about someone alleging that they had met Jesus Christ in person. In the book, the author claimed that Jesus actually materialized in front of him on an almost daily basis. Spiritually, I was greatly disturbed. As I read it, I sensed that the author had falsified many of the accounts. I also sensed an agenda that was not God-ordained. The emphasis was on him, not the Lord whom he claimed visited him often. I relayed this to Mother Brown. She advised me to stop reading it. Her reason: evil spirits can attach themselves to books.

I found out later that the writer of this particular book had sexual encounters with various women, some of whom I know personally. Pictures and screenshots of sexually explicit text messages were sent to me by them. There were other allegations that I won't reveal here. I became aware, by means of discernment, that this individual was involved in sexual sin while writing his book. That spirit had impregnated the book, permitting demons to be birthed out of the pages and manifest in the lives of the readers.

A Deliverance Book Full of Demons

On another occasion—a relatively calm summer evening—I was lying in bed reading a book on deliverance. When I finished it, something peculiar and frightening happened. As I found myself between wakefulness and slumber, I felt something on top of me! I couldn't see it, but I could feel its weight. It had a presence, but no physical body. I immediately called upon the name of my Lord and Savior, Jesus Christ, and felt this thing start to slide down my body. I was relieved because I thought my ordeal was over, but to my dismay, it wasn't! This monster jumped back on my chest! I was being spiritually crushed under the pressure of an invisible force!

I called on my Lord a second time, but this time, I spoke with the authority of a believer, "In the name of Jesus," I declared, "get off me!"

Not surprisingly, it made a hasty exit.

Afterward, I was perplexed. What had just happened? One thing I knew was that it was a demon, but I couldn't figure out what caused it to attack me. Subsequently, I asked my wife to read the same book. Don't judge me, people! I wasn't sure that the book was the cause of the attack. I thought that it might have been all in my head.

The next night, my wife, Elisa, positioned herself on the couch in our living room, reading the same book I'd read the previous evening. Later, after finishing a majority of the text, she fell asleep. That morning she reported that something invisible sat on her during the night and wouldn't allow her to move. She rebuked it in Jesus's name, and it was gone.

In response to this revelation, I grabbed the book while my wife was away, threw it in our bathroom tub and set it on fire. Upon her return, her reaction was not pleasant because I damaged the tub. In my zeal to rid our home of this book that I understood to be occupied by devils, I didn't think about the potential damage. But it worked! We didn't experience that type of attack again.

Test Every Book's Spirit

To this day, I'm extremely guarded concerning the type of reading material I allow in my house. They have to go through rigorous spiritual scrutiny before I allow the text to permeate my eye gates, and you should do likewise.

We must test every spirit to see whether it be from the Lord, even when choosing the literature we read. Books that originate from Satan are loaded with demons with orders to infiltrate our minds and bodies. When you read a book, you're opening your spirit up to the contents written within. Spirits can and will enter you the longer you regale or entertain them.

WHY THE DEVIL ATTACKS THROUGH CERTAIN BOOKS

I've never seen deliverance services where they cast out demons that come from books. Have you ever had an ominous feeling during or after reading certain books? I believe this occurs for two reasons:

1. The book may be of the Lord and the devil attacks you because he doesn't want you to find out information and revelation contained within that could do damage to his kingdom.

2. The book is of a satanic origin and was written expressly with an evil agenda in mind.

1. The book is of the Lord.

It was around 4:30 p.m. when I suddenly got the urge to go to a local Christian bookstore. In my spirit, I heard the Lord tell me that He had something there for me. As I endeavored to go, the phone kept ringing amid other distractions. Fifteen minutes had passed. It was now 4:45 p.m. and the bookstore closes at 5:00 p.m. The continued attempts to keep me from going only strengthened my resolve to go. My thought process was, "If the devil is fighting this hard to keep me here, then there must be something he doesn't want me to have there." Somehow, I managed to run out the door and made it to the store at exactly 4:55 p.m. with only five minutes to spare!

I hurriedly examined the books on the shelves and came across one that immediately grabbed my attention. It was titled *101 Questions and Answers on Demon Powers* by Lester Frank Sumrall.[3] I hurried home, anticipating how this book would bless me.

The next morning, I recounted the story to Elisa. She asked to see the book. I gave it to her and she opened it up randomly. It landed on a page that dealt with commonly used playing cards, triggering a memory for her. My wife ran to our closet and pulled out a deck of tarot cards! Tarot cards are used to foresee future events, answer specific questions, and for fortune-telling and astrology. They are of satanic origin and utilized by practitioners in the dark arts. These demonic cards should not be in your home. A tarot deck is usually made up of seventy-eight cards, each with a unique image and meaning. Had I not gone out to get that book the previous night, we may never have realized that they were there. The cards were destroyed and discarded straightaway.

Before she made Jesus Christ the Lord of her life, my wife hung with coworkers who were deeply involved in occult practices. Based on my prior knowledge and experience with tarot cards (see my book, *Supernaturally Prophetic*), I warned her of the consequences of participating in such activities with her colleagues. Once we were in relationship with the Lord, she stopped associating with them and renounced all ungodly activity. If you've had the same or similar experiences, it's imperative that you repent and abandon any occultic involvement in Jesus's name. The Lord will forgive and cleanse you.

This whole story taught me a couple of lessons:

1. Every blessing may not be directly for you, but it can bless you indirectly.

2. The Lord can use a book to undo demonic strongholds and close portals.

Playing with tarot cards is an entry point for demons. Once we destroyed the cards, that door was shut. Let's move on to my next point about why you may get a bad feeling during or after reading certain books.

2. The book is of satanic origin.

As a teenager, not only was I attracted to spiritual and paranormal books, but I also enjoyed real-life crime stories that included graphic details of murders, assaults, and other types of criminal actions. These books and others like them have obvious roots in the works of the flesh described in Galatians 5.

My late father, Dr. Andre Dunigan, used to warn me against reading such books, stating that the content could get into my spirit. He warned of possibly duplicating the atrocious acts within the novels. When I started getting revelation concerning the things of the spirit, I realized that he was correct. Much of the anger and rebellion that lived inside me and in my childhood home had a direct connection to the books I read. As I read them, I opened the door for the enemy to torment my life.

Books that originate in darkness are cursed and should have no place in a believer's life. You can't expect to be blessed living with cursed things. They will keep you from winning battles that could have been easily won.

How to Test the Spirits of the Books You Read

I wanted to explain this to you so you won't burn up every book you read based on a feeling. Some books may be godly, while others are not. You must be able to discern (perceive) the difference. In fact, the gift of discernment will be one of your greatest weapons in preventing these spirits from becoming an issue.

If you listen to the Holy Spirit, He will guide and direct in terms of what you should or shouldn't read. Listen to His instructions and obey Him when deciding what reading material to select.

The first thing you should do to test the spirit of the book is research the author. Whatever spirit(s) is in him or her will more than likely be present within their writings. You can do this via the World Wide Web, making inquiries of those who know the author personally or by asking the Lord directly. To do the latter, you must be familiar with God's voice. When you know His voice, you'll be able to hear and distinguish it when choosing books.

Whatever you read has the potential to affect and infect you, for either good or evil. Be very careful about what you allow your eyes to entertain. Every book has a spirit that you must discern.

CHAPTER 7

UNCLEAN SPIRITS AND CURSED OBJECTS:
SIN IN THE CAMP

Let's turn now to the Word and examine the sin of Achan in Joshua 7. His story is a prime example of how serious God is about us keeping our homes, our lives, and objects we possess free from unclean spirits.

ACHAN: THE ONE WHO TROUBLES

The name *Achan* means "one who troubles" and "to besmirch (to stain or sully): change in a negative manner or he that troubleth."[1] The son of Carmi, he was known as the one "who brought disaster on Israel by taking plunder that had been set apart for the Lord" (1 Chron. 2:7, NLT).[2]

In Joshua chapters 7 and 8, the people of Israel engaged in two battles in an attempt to conquer the Canaanite city, Ai. In the first attempt (see Josh. 7), they lost the battle partly because they were arrogant. Their conceit was evidenced by their choice to not thoroughly consult God before facing Ai, as they did in the battle of

Jericho prior. If they had, I'm sure the Lord would have let them know that it was a battle that they wouldn't win. The fault lay in underestimating their enemy. Israel was looking at the smallness of Ai, only bringing two to three thousand men to war at the behest of the spies sent to Ai (see Josh. 7:2). They told Joshua not to take the whole army because the people of Ai were few (see Josh. 7:3). We're told in Second Corinthians 5:7 to walk by faith and not by sight, but in this case, the Israelites did the opposite.

Joshua and the children of Israel lost to Ai (see Josh. 7:4), an exceptionally small army they should have easily defeated, especially since the Lord of hosts was on their side.

In the scriptures that follow, Joshua tries to make sense of this devastating loss by inquiring of the Lord. This was His response:

> *Israel hath sinned, and they have also transgressed my covenant which I commanded them: for they have even taken of the accursed thing, and have also stolen, and dissembled also, and they have put it even among their own stuff.*
>
> *Therefore the children of Israel could not stand before their enemies, but turned their backs before their enemies, because they were accursed: neither will I be with you any more, except ye destroy the accursed from among you* (Joshua 7:11-12).

After drawing lots and determining that Achan was the accursed within their camp, he, his family, and the stolen goods were all destroyed. This had to be done in order to assure victory in their next engagement against Ai in Joshua 8.

When you bring something into your house that the Lord doesn't approve of, demons may acquire entrance. As previously mentioned, after I'd received the revelation about the nature of what I had brought into our home, I got rid of the books! As we've learned from Achan, disobedience can bring on a curse. I highly recommend that when you discover cursed merchandise in your home, get it out right away. You must get rid of your Achans, which is anything or anyone who curses your life. Let's look at some of the traits of an Achan.

CHARACTERISTICS OF ACHANS

In order to see the victory of God reactivated in your life—do an Achan check! You must in order to get the Achans out of your life, so that you won't experience demonic weight that will hinder successful living in Him ("Lay aside every weight and sin" [Heb. 12:1]).

Here are some characteristics of Achans that will help you spot them easier. Achans will:

- Steal from your life (time, talent, treasure)
- Hide what was stolen
- Only confess their sin when confronted
- Use you to get into places to steal
- Hold things back from you
- Curse your life until you remove them
- Impede your progress

I am not advocating that you burn up and destroy the people in your life whom you feel are cursing it, just the inanimate objects. When you steal items and place them among your personal possessions, the cursed or stolen objects have the potential to contaminate the blessed ones due to their proximity. The cursed books that I stole as a teenager literally and spiritually infected everything in our living space that was not committed to the Lord, very similar to a human virus. If I only knew then what I know now, those instruments of Lucifer would not have gained entry into our home.

THE DEVIL'S TROJAN HORSE

The devil will use a Trojan horse of sorts to get into your camp. Do you remember the story of the Trojan horse? According to Webopedia.com, "The term comes from the story of the Trojan War, in which the Greeks give a giant wooden horse to their foes, the Trojans, ostensibly as a peace offering. But after the Trojans drag the horse inside their city walls, Greek soldiers sneak out of the horse's hollow belly and open the city gates, allowing their compatriots to pour in and capture Troy."[3]

This is a precise description of demonic infiltration! They come appearing as something else in order to get you to drop your guard and let them in. Once in, they leave the vehicle they hid in and make residence in your house or even in you!

The Trojans probably looked upon this giant, wooden horse as a blessing and eagerly pulled it into their gates. They unwittingly gave their enemies, the Greeks, authorization to invade by permitting the horse (the gift) to be ushered in their gates.

Remember, demons need permission to enter your body. This can happen through an active will or inactive will. Simply, this means that some people invite devils in, while others allow them in through spiritual misadventure. The latter gives satanic emissaries access by doing exactly what I did—bringing something that's cursed by God into their home due to spiritual blindness or ignorance.

To rid your house of potential incoming spirits, you have to remove the cursed items from your place and destroy them. Not doing so results in most battles in the spirit and the natural to be lost. Some don't realize that a Trojan horse is in their midst. This is due to the idolization of satanic gifts (objects) without realizing it.

In my view, the horse was looked upon not just as a potential gift, but also as an idol to be worshiped. It was presumably large and had a commanding presence, just the type of hulk to be revered by the people. Please understand that anything you idolize above God contains a demonic component. Remember also that behind every idol there is a demon.

> *They provoked him to jealousy with strange gods, with abominations provoked they him to anger. They sacrificed unto devils, not to God; to gods whom they knew not, to new gods that came newly up, whom your fathers feared not* (Deuteronomy 32:16-17).

In the New Testament, we are admonished to stay away from idols. Biblically, this applies to all idols.

> *Little children, keep* [guard] *yourselves from idols. Amen* (1 John 5:21).

DESTROY THE ACCURSED THINGS

In order for Joshua and the children of Israel to win any other battles, the accursed things, including the accursed people, had to be destroyed. Once you have a cursed object in your possession, you and yours can become cursed as well; at least this was the case in Old Testament times. It may be so in current times as well if you're not properly covered by the precious blood of Jesus Christ, our Lord.

When confronted, Achan confessed his sin. He was summarily taken, along with his loved ones, livestock, home, and the cursed merchandise. Achan and his family were stoned to death by all of Israel and set on fire. Did the others in the camp want to do this? Probably not, but the Most High told them to. Then and only then, after Achan, his family, and all that he possessed were eliminated, was the wrath of the Lord satiated.

> *Then Joshua, together with all Israel, took Achan son of Zerah, the silver, the robe, the gold bar, his sons and daughters, his cattle, donkeys and sheep, his tent and all that he had, to the Valley of Achor. Joshua said, "Why have you brought this trouble on us? The Lord will bring trouble on you today."*
>
> *Then all Israel stoned him, and after they had stoned the rest, they burned them. Over Achan they heaped up a large pile of rocks, which remains to this day. Then the Lord turned from his fierce anger. Therefore that place has been called the Valley of Achor ever since* (Joshua 7:24-26, NIV).

THE ACCURSED HAS AN ODOR

As I related to you earlier, when I brought the *Trojan horse* (accursed things) into my house, very peculiar things begin to happen that horrified my family and myself. The first incident happened while I was in the kitchen sitting at our table, eating, and my mom was standing, washing the dishes. All of a sudden, an unearthly smell permeated the room. Before I could allow any words to pass from my lips concerning this foul odor, my flabbergasted mother yelled out, "What is that smell?"

Comforted in the fact that I hadn't lost my mind since she had detected it too, I hastily replied, "I don't know!"

To describe the smell as ghastly is a huge understatement. This reeking odor was likened to decaying flesh, feces, vomit, urine, and every other malodorous (smelly) thing that you can think of magnified a hundred times! As I mentioned before, whatever or wherever this originated from was not of this world. *The stench literally had a presence*! Just by the odor, I could tell its location. It seemed to come up from our basement, go through the kitchen, between my mother and me, and out the back door.

Have you ever had someone walk by you with cologne or perfume on? You only catch a whiff of it, and then it's gone. We smelled it only for only a moment and then the evil presence was gone. My mom and I stared at each other in disbelief. What was that?

John 11:39 gives us a clue. Anything that's dead stinks: "he [Lazarus] stinketh: for he hath been dead four days." Demons are spiritually dead in terms of being alive to the Lord, so they have a smell that can be experienced in the spirit and sometimes in the natural.

It's my sincere assessment that the entity that walked through our kitchen was a demon allowed in through the books I brought into our home. These writings invited devils into our dwelling.

BE CAREFUL WHAT YOU BRING HOME

We all must be incredibly careful in what we permit in our homes. The following bears repeating—discerning of spirits, one of the nine gifts of the Spirit, is very useful in determining what to bring in and what to keep out. There are some of you who are reading this book right now who naïvely brought idols into your households.

> *What do I imply then? That food offered to idols is anything, or that an idol is anything? No, I imply that what pagans sacrifice they offer to demons and not to God. I do not want you to be participants with demons* (1 Corinthians 10:19-20, ESV).

Idol is "a representation or symbol of an object of worship; *broadly*: a false god." It is "a likeness of something; a "pretender, impostor."[4]

Anything we idolize or place above God can and will be taken away from us. Idols can become gods in our lives. First Corinthians 10:19-20, referenced above, provides evidence that supports my previous statement that behind every idol is a demon. So, when we worship idols, we're really worshiping the evil spirit behind it. The Lord will not tolerate this, especially from His people. He says, in Deuteronomy 5:7, "Thou shalt have none other gods before me."

We can unintentionally place other gods before God. Believe it or not, these false gods can include television, food, ministry, celebrities, and even our children. Yes, we can idolize our kids by loving them more than we love the Lord. Whether we realize it or not, Christian ministry can sometimes be placed above the Lord of our lives. If it replaces the time spent with God and family, ministry can become an idol. I've seen marriages wrecked because a husband made ministry his mistress. He spent more time with his ministers than his wife and children. This is definitely not the will of God. A recommended order of priorities in life should be the Lord first, family second, and ministry third. Any deviation of this order can cause an imbalance.

In conclusion, don't allow an idol to rule your life. Numerous people embrace idols without realizing that they're holding on to the demons behind and in them. This provides evil spirits admittance into your home. The goal of the entities is to disrupt, dismantle, and destroy your life. Don't let them! Identify the accursed thing, cast it out, and destroy it.

PART III

GETTING FREE

CHAPTER 8

THE AUTHORITY OF A BELIEVER

Behold, I give unto you power to tread on serpents
and scorpions, and over all the power of the
enemy: and nothing shall by any means hurt you.
—LUKE 10:19

By 1998, I was married. My wife, Elisa, and I lived in a petite, single-bedroom attic that had been converted into an apartment—still on the South Side of Chicago. Just slightly bigger than a studio apartment, our place was so tiny that if you tripped in the bedroom, you ended up in the living room. If you stumbled in the living room, you wound up in the kitchen. But the rent was cheap, and we were (and still are) deeply in love.

Thirteen years before this, in 1985, I had accepted Jesus Christ as my Lord and Savior, but found myself in a backslidden position soon afterward. For those thirteen years, I had a form of godliness and denied God's power. But now (1985), an unquenchable fire began to burn in my heart for the power of God to become active in my life. I went after it with everything I had.

I was also working on a master's degree in special education at the time, which required quite a bit of late-night study. One evening, I was in the living room, preparing for an exam the next day. My wife was fast asleep in our bedroom with the door closed. All of a sudden, I felt this strong urge to check on her. I got up from my studies and went to our room. As I went in, I noticed that it was unnaturally dark and had a foreboding feel to it. I looked toward my spouse, sleeping peacefully in our bed, and noticed a figure in the room. Now this "thing" appeared to be about three feet tall and black in color. Its outline was visible because of a combination of the street lights and moonlight that entered in through the bedroom window. The *trespasser* had no noticeable hair, a slender build, and blurred facial features. It was standing, but slightly bent over, near my wife's head, speaking to her. I couldn't make out what it was saying, yet I knew it was talking to my wife as she slept. The conversation was definitely one-sided!

When I came into the room, it seemed startled. It appeared to leer at me, then quickly disappeared. I searched the room thoroughly, but found no one. My wife slept through the whole thing. I noticed that before I had an opportunity to rebuke it in Jesus's name it left. It's my belief that as believers, we carry the authority of Jesus even before we use His name. The name above all names is branded upon us, spiritually, the moment we accept Christ as Lord. In Scripture, when individuals were brought to Peter, some believed that even his shadow could actually heal them! This happened even before Peter had the chance to speak the wonderful name of the Lord.

> *Insomuch that they brought forth the sick into the streets, and laid them on beds and couches, that at the least the shadow of Peter passing by might overshadow some of them* (Acts 5:15).

Don't misunderstand me—there is sufficient power in the name of Jesus, but sometimes devils will flee because they see Christ in you, the hope of glory!

When that devil saw me, he wasn't afraid of me per se, but he was terrified of the Lord within me! Instead of seeing only me, it saw the Holy Spirit in me because of my submission to God. This submission, along with resistance, equals a demonic exodus (exit)!

During this same time, I can remember feeling something sitting on me at night too. I would often feel it to the point of immobilization. Whenever I called on the name of Jesus, it left. This happened numerous times. As mentioned in Chapter 6, a demon pounced on my chest while I lay in bed. I rebuked it in Jesus's name and felt it slide down my body, then abruptly jump on my chest again! I pleaded the blood against it, but this time with the authority of a believer, and it finally left.

New Believer, Fresh Meat

Attacks such as these are not uncommon to true believers, especially when they initially and sincerely accept Jesus Christ into their lives. This is when the enemy launches a full-fledged assault against new Christians in an attempt to scare them back into a life of sin. I compare this attack to a bigger country going to war with a smaller country that it sees as a potential threat. The goal is to dominate the smaller country before it can become a legitimate superpower.

That's how the devil views a novice Christian. It's the reason why the intimidation efforts are so robust (strong) at the beginning. Most of my supernatural occurrences took place when I first got saved, and they did not happen by chance or coincidence. The hordes of hell strategically planned each assault in their futile effort to get me to stop running for Jesus.

They will usually leave you alone when you're not serious and totally sold out to a life lived in total surrender to the King. The devil won't waste energy bothering people he thinks he already has. Demons watch you and can somehow perceive when you really mean business with God. If you are not playing when it comes to your walk with Him, don't be alarmed when demonic attacks become more severe. Truth be told, it's a backward compliment from the enemy. If you weren't a threat to the kingdom of darkness, then he wouldn't be messing with you!

RUN TOWARD THE BATTLE

Satan is a coward who will assail you at the point he feels you're most vulnerable. This could happen during the death of a cherished loved one, sickness, or in the midst of a financial crisis. He's so low down that even your children are not off-limits. If he can't get through the hedge of protection given to you by the Lord, Lucifer will come against those you love most. In these times, you must remember that the devil fights hard, but he doesn't fight long.

I have been harassed by demons multiple times over the years, but God has supernaturally delivered me from the spirit of fear whenever Satan attacks me now. The closer I am to Him, the less distress I have in dealing with the devil's assaults. The more he confronts me, the more I confront him. Satan's aggression toward me is an indicator that I'm on the right track. The more he attempts to stop my progress, the more I press into my God-given assignment.

Just like when David confronted Goliath in Scripture, you must run toward the enemy, not away from him. (See First Samuel 17:48.) Young David ran toward the giant to engage him in a battle that looked awfully one-sided in favor of Goliath. It wasn't that David thought he could beat Goliath by himself. He had confidence in the One who sent him into war. The future king and prophet placed all his confidence in the Lord and knew the outcome before the battle. Though many doubted his victory, he never did. David possessed the God-kind of confidence and so should we when facing Satan. It exists when you allow His confidence in you to overcome your confidence in yourself.

Satan is a defeated foe because of the finished work of Jesus Christ on the cross at Calvary. There is no need for any type of phobia on your part when facing him or his minions. According to Luke 10:19, Jesus gave you dominion over the evil one and his soldiers.

Nothing, not one single thing can hurt you because you, as a Christian, have been empowered by Christ! Remember this when facing powers that want to keep you bound to the will of devils. According to the verse at the beginning of this chapter, the devil (serpent) and his demons (scorpions) are under your feet! The Most High has given you power over them, so why be afraid of the demonic forces that come against you? You don't have to be. Through faith and the use of His name, you too can be supernaturally delivered.

CHAPTER 9

SELF-DELIVERANCE

And when he had called unto him his twelve disciples, he gave them power against unclean spirits, to cast them out, and to heal all manner of sickness and all manner of disease.
—MATTHEW 10:1

Self-deliverance means exactly what the name suggests—delivering yourself by the power, authority, and name of Jesus Christ. It can be done through prayer, worship, or just calling out any foreign spiritual bodies you feel have taken up residence within you. Now this may not work in every situation involving casting devils out of yourself. It really depends on the level of infestation and the strength of the demons. If you find that some spirits are not loosening their grip as you pray and renounce their authority over your life, it's good practice to seek out a seasoned, anointed, and proven minster of deliverance.

In one of the best books that I've ever read on the subject, *Pigs in the Parlor: A Practical Guide to Deliverance*, authors Frank and

Ida Mae Hammond wrote, "After a person has experienced an initial deliverance at the hands of an experienced minister, he can begin to practice self-deliverance."[1]

Before you can self-deliver, you must get delivered! Satan can't cast out Satan. I have heard so many tragic stories of people with devils attempting to administer deliverance to infected individuals. In other words, the deliverance ministers actually needed deliverance before they could be effective in delivering others! Acts 19:13-16 tells the cautionary and true tale of the seven sons of Sceva who attempted and failed horribly at casting devils out of a demonized man. They tried to evict the demons by using the name of Jesus whom Paul preached, but they had no personal relationship with Christ. Somehow, they thought they could use His name without knowing Him. What they failed to realize is that when you don't have an intimate affiliation with Jesus Christ, you are prohibited access to His influence, power, and clout that make their home in His prodigious name.

In verse 15, the evil spirit questioned the influence, lineage (in relation to the Lord), and pedagogy (training) of these vagabond, Jewish exorcists, saying, "Jesus, I know, and Paul I know; but who are ye?" The next verse states that the possessed individual leapt on them, overcame them, and prevailed against them, so that they fled out of that house, naked and wounded.

Can you imagine being pummeled (beaten) so severely that you lose your clothes? Well, this is what happens to many people who toy with deliverance or are insecure in their own position and authority in Christ.

What happened to the seven sons of Sceva teaches us that we cannot rely on others' involvement or relationship with Jesus. We must diligently cultivate our own familiarity in order to walk in the power of His might when facing the adversary.

My own foray into self-deliverance was clumsy and embarrassing at some points and downright dreadful in others. Yet, the Lord brought me through those experiences to strengthen me for battle and to increase my ability to discern the enemy long before he made his move. I see every experience as a stepping stone to the supernatural deliverance and anointing that I walk in today.

NOT LIKE THE EXORCIST

As stated earlier, I had an interest in deliverance ministry since I first received Jesus Christ as Lord in 1985. Ever since I was a child, I had a proclivity toward anything supernatural. I'd feel a sense of wonder when anyone brought the topic up. I truly became serious about my walk with God in 1998 and devoured every book I could get my hands on in reference to casting out devils. Books by Frank and Ida Mae Hammond, Win Worley, Ruth Brown, and John Eckhardt were plenteous in my library. I just knew this was my calling and needed as much information and revelation as possible to prepare me for it.

I had seen movies like *The Exorcist* and supposed that was what deliverance ministry looked like—the demonized person spitting up green pea soup, head spinning around, and so on. Hollywood really overexaggerated the entire methodology and manifestations of the ministry. Still, I sought to understand what casting out devils actually entailed.

Ask Them What?

One day I came across a book in which a woman of God spoke about having a multitude of demons cast out of her. I was so enthralled by it that I ordered two cassette tapes (that's how long ago it was!)—a self-deliverance recording and the actual deliverance session the author was involved in before writing her book. I listened to the latter first. This cassette featured a room full of people getting delivered from an abundance of foul entities. The language that emitted from them sounded like literal hell on earth! I had never heard anything human make noises like that. As I continued to listen, chills ran up and down my spine, and fear made a sincere attempt to claim me.

On the tape, the facilitating pastor asked the demons that inhabited the author a series of questions, allowing them to answer. There were way too many inquiries made of the devils for my taste. I was always taught that you should not ask demons an assortment of questions. I was so grieved by what I heard that I called the author (her number was in the book) and asked her, "Should you be asking demons questions?"

She replied, "Why, yes! That's how you get information out of them."

I was shocked! Ask devils—master manipulators, tricksters, and liars—a lot of questions to get the truth out of them? Well, "Jesus didn't do it, so I'm not either!" was the attitude I adopted after our conversation. I will elaborate more on this topic in Chapter 10.

JUST GET THEM OUT!

When dealing with devils, statements should override or outnumber inquiries, because the more you interrogate them, the longer they'll stay in the person's body. For example, if your boss at work called you into his office to talk, you'd likely stay until he finished his queries, right? If you were headed toward the exit to leave his or her office and they asked a question, you would stop to answer it, correct? I hope you're able to see where I'm going with this.

As a deliverance minister or believer, you have authority over demons in the name of Jesus Christ. While trying to cast out a devil, as long as you're asking it to divulge more information, it won't go. When ministering deliverance to anyone, make more statements than questions. The questions, if any, that you ask should always be Holy Spirit-led. I didn't heed the author's advice, though I do value her testimony and ministry.

WE STARTED WITH US

Another series of cassette tapes that I was immensely excited to utilize were directly related to self-deliverance. I convinced my wife to join me on this excursion into unknown territory. She reluctantly agreed. So, we retrieved the instructions that came with the tapes, and we both got in the bed, ready to cast out some devils! I read the instructions aloud so that she could hear. They clearly indicated that we needed to be vigilant of any violent manifestations that could occur during the process. Basically, they were instructing us not to be surprised if we start growling, screaming, behaving unusually, or had voices come out of us that sounded nothing like our own.

My thoughts went along these lines: "I don't have any devils! My wife may have some, but not me!" I was far too anointed to have a demon, right? Besides, I was a super Christian, with a big C on my chest in the spirit! My wife had only just recently accepted Jesus Christ as Lord and Savior. She must have something.

These are terrible thoughts, right? In my defense, I was a newly recommitted Christian, full of fire, zeal, and unfortunately, religion. By this, I mean that I had *caught* a religious spirit that was a little like the Pharisees of the New Testament.

With my religious thoughts in tow, I put the cassette in a small portable player. My wife and I shared one set of earphones, one in her ear and the other in my own. Note: we were pretty poor at the time. The tape began to play, and the gravelly voice of a seasoned man of God came on. He repeated the instructions we had previously read and began the session by calling out numerous names of demonic spirits such as anger, fear, lust, pride, gluttony, and others.

About twenty minutes into the audio, I began to feel strange. My heart started to race, and anxiety gripped my very being! I alerted my wife to my unexpected condition, and she slowly, but deliberately, eased her way off the bed and away from me. *Thanks, honey!* To my surprise and alarm, a demon that was in me was manifesting! With great trepidation, I continued to listen to the tape (alone at this point) all the way to its conclusion.

Guess what? I got delivered from something. Though I am still not exactly sure what it was, by the end of the night I felt completely free. I wept and gave God the glory for it!

ANYONE CAN HAVE A DEMON

This encounter taught me that anyone could have a demon, even a Christian. I was a sold-out, born-again believer in Jesus Christ, yet I apparently had a devil or devils. How did it or they get in? What did I do to cause this? Was I really saved? These questions and others danced around in my head for quite some time afterward. Later, I learned that evil spirits gain entry to believers through their flesh, either by *ancestry, accident,* or *acceptance.* This simply means that some devils are inherited through generational curses, tragic mistakes, or openings caused by willful, consistent, and sinful behavior on our part. I'm not saying that these are the only avenues by which they enter. There are others. I relegate the previous three options to my own personal knowledge and understanding.

Though demons can get in the body of a believer, they cannot possess a Christian; possession denotes ownership. If you are Holy Ghost-filled, then you belong to the Lord. Once you belong to God, Satan cannot *own* you. Demons can *oppress* you, but they can never *possess* you!

Sickness and Demonic Oppression

Sickness can have its origins in the demonic. In the following Scripture, notice that Jesus cast the evil spirits out of people *before* He healed them!

> *When the even was come, they brought unto him many that were possessed with devils: and he cast out the spirits with his word, and healed all that were sick* (Matthew 8:16).

I truly believe demons are responsible for most illnesses, either directly or indirectly. They can influence you into consuming foods on a consistent basis that cause bad health (that is, fast food, processed foods, and the like). Demons that come in through rejection, trauma, and abuse can inspire a person to emotionally eat. This may cause them to consume far too many unhealthy foods in search of comfort and joy. Essentially, these people feed the shame that they are hoping to escape. On the other end of this, demons that encourage overeating can also be connected to demons of suicide, as the person slowly eats his or her self into an early grave. This is also where devils can implant themselves in individuals' bodies disguised as cancer, diabetes, high blood pressure, heart disease, and more.

Deliverance from these demons results in healing sometimes without addressing the specific illness. Some people are instantaneously healed after a self-deliverance session, while others require an experienced minister to do it. This is needed when the devils are stubborn and securely dug into the host, refusing to come out. What Jesus did in Matthew 8:16 bears revisiting here: He cast out the devils first, then healed everyone who was infirmed.

In John 5, Jesus healed a man who had an infirmity for thirty-eight years. This man stayed in his condition because he didn't have anyone to place him in the Pool of Bethesda (place of healing), which the angels troubled (stirred) at various times. Now and then, depending on others can hinder the expediency of your healing or deliverance. As we see within the verses below, you can't rely upon someone else throwing you into the pool!

For an angel went down at a certain season into the
pool, and troubled the water: whosoever then first

after the troubling of the water stepped in was made whole of whatsoever disease he had.

And a certain man was there, which had an infirmity thirty and eight years. When Jesus saw him lie, and knew that he had been now a long time in that case, he saith unto him, Wilt thou be made whole?

The impotent man answered him, Sir, I have no man, when the water is troubled, to put me into the pool: but while I am coming, another steppeth down before me.

Jesus saith unto him, Rise, take up thy bed, and walk (John 5:4-8).

Self-deliverance can be a valid alternative for those who can't find anyone to throw them into the pool. An apostle whom I have great respect for, once told me that if that same sick individual had just rolled himself over twice a year in the direction of the healing waters, he would have been able to reach the Pool of Bethesda and throw himself in! In other words, don't wait on people when you need devils cast out of you. Your total dependence must be placed upon the Lord. He will show you what vehicle (self-deliverance or a deliverance minister) to use to get free.

MAINTAIN SPIRITUAL HEALTH THROUGH REGULAR SELF-DELIVERANCE

My late spiritual mother, Ruth Brown, the author of *Destroying the Works of Witchcraft through Fasting and Prayer*, always did deliverance on herself.[2] In fact, she did so on a weekly basis. She was the most anointed woman of God I've ever known. Mother

Ruthie, as she was affectionately called by friends and family, constantly wanted to get rid of anything that was in her that was not of the Lord. She habitually performed a spiritual inventory on herself, with added housecleaning. This is something we all should do unswervingly to maintain the spiritual health of our "homes." The homes, being our bodies, which are the temples of the Holy Spirit (see 1 Cor. 6:19).

When Jesus healed this impotent man, he stated in John 5:14, "Behold, thou art made whole: sin no more, lest a worse thing come unto thee." In this verse, Jesus infers that sin caused the man's impotency for the past thirty-eight years. So that means that sin brought on illness in this instance. We must also grasp that sickness is a spirit that can be rebuked or cast out. I'll expound on an example of this in reference to Simon's mother in Chapter 10.

There is a demon called sickness that you can get delivered from. Your freedom can come through self-deliverance. I've witnessed this myself. There have been people who cast out spirits of infirmity lodged in their bodies using the name of Jesus. They were supernaturally delivered from sickness!

PART IV

CALLED TO DELIVER

CHAPTER 10

DELIVERANCE 101: THE BASICS

*And these signs shall follow them that believe;
in my name shall they cast out devils; they
shall speak with new tongues; they shall take
up serpents; and if they drink any deadly
thing, it shall not hurt them; they shall lay
hands on the sick, and they shall recover.*
—MARK 16:17-18

Deliverance in Hebrew is *peleytah* or *peletah*, which means "escape" or "who have escaped."[1] The English word *deliver* is defined as the following:

1. To set free
2. To assist in giving birth
3. To give birth to
4. To come through[2]

The goal of deliverance can be summed up in the following verse:

> *But when people keep on sinning, it shows that they belong to the devil, who has been sinning since the beginning. But the Son of God came to destroy the works of the devil* (1 John 3:8, NLT).

While in the flesh, Jesus came to earth to destroy the vocations of the devil! He did this through personally ministering deliverance and teaching His disciples to do the same. The goal of every deliverance worker should be to pass on their knowledge of casting out demons to the next generation. The enemy hates the perpetuation of deliverance ministry and will always try to stop such dissemination.

Throughout the New Testament, hell was referred to more than heaven. When Jesus gave the signs that would follow believers, casting out demons was at the top of the list. This gives even more credibility to the importance of deliverance ministry.

Spirits of Infirmity Can Be Cast Out

As discussed earlier, in order to eradicate some sicknesses, demons must be cast out before healing can take place. All sickness is not caused by demons. Though I attribute Satan as the author of illness, some are brought on through our own doing. In Galatians 6:7, we are told that we will reap what we sow. For example, if we continue in maintaining an unhealthy diet, then infirmity would likely be the outcome. The phrase "you are what you eat" is justifiable here. When an ailment's origin is found within the spiritual realm, then it can be cast out in the natural, as evidenced in the following Scripture.

> *And he arose out of the synagogue, and entered into Simon's house. And Simon's wife's mother was taken with a great fever; and they besought him for her. And he [Jesus] stood over her, and rebuked the fever; and it left her: and immediately she arose and ministered unto them* (Luke 4:38-39).

How could Jesus rebuke the fever? He was able to do so because it was a spirit of infirmity. As a spirit, it can be driven out. We have that same power. Spirits can and will be driven out when rebuked in faith, in His name. He did the same thing in Luke 13 with the woman with a spirit of infirmity. First, Jesus loosed the woman from the spirit, and then He laid hands on her for healing. The following verses demonstrate the emphasis the Lord places on healing and deliverance. The two go hand in hand. I'll elaborate on this more in Chapter 12.

> *And as ye go, preach, saying, The kingdom of heaven is at hand. Heal the sick, cleanse the lepers, raise the dead, cast out devils: freely ye have received, freely give* (Matthew 10:7-8).
>
> *And the people with one accord gave heed unto those things which Philip spake, hearing and seeing the miracles which he did.*
>
> *For unclean spirits, crying with loud voice, came out of many that were possessed with them: and many taken with palsies, and that were lame, were healed. And there was great joy in that city* (Acts 8:6-8).

You Don't Have to Yell

When casting out demons, please speak calmly, yet sternly. You don't have to yell and scream at demons to get them to leave a person. You'll end up leaving the victimized individual with *deafness* instead of *deliverance*! It's not about your volume, but it's about the power and authority only found in the name of Jesus! Rest assured, demons can hear you, even if you whisper.

I heard a story about one apostolic general who likened casting out demons to a dog and his master. He said that if your family dog follows you and you don't want him to, saying very passively to your pet, "Go home," probably won't work very well. But if say those same two words with authority and power, your dog will more than likely follow your commands. This is how Christians should address demons in order to get them to leave.

Demonic Houses and Doors

When someone dies while being inhabited by demons, Satan's representatives will quickly look for another domicile. Remember, they view human bodies as potential homes. Those same demons have a tendency to stay within the family. In fact, they will search for relatives who have given or are willing to give themselves over to their specific satanic assignment. For example, a demon of perversion will enter another family member who already has a perverse spirit. Why? Because there's already a breach or opening in them. Not only do they enter, but they bring along seven more spirits more wicked than themselves. The perverse spirit that already lives there will open the door for the others.

When the unclean spirit is gone out of a man, he walketh through dry places, seeking rest, and findeth none.

Then he saith, I will return into my house from whence I came out; and when he is come, he findeth it empty, swept, and garnished.

Then goeth he, and taketh with himself seven other spirits more wicked than himself, and they enter in and dwell there: and the last state of that man is worse than the first. Even so shall it be also unto this wicked generation (Matthew 12:43-45).

I believe that "my house," referred to in Matthew 12:43 above, doesn't just apply to one person, but their whole family. *Merriam-Webster's Dictionary* defines *house* as "a building that serves as living quarters for one or a few families."[3] According to their definition, one home can hold one or a few family members. This leads me to the conclusion that when a demon returns to his dwelling place with his friends, he has the option of invading anyone within that abode who is open to him. As I mentioned earlier, "open" refers to specific family members who have personally sinned or freely allowed themselves to be used for demonic penetration.

Habitual sin can be an open door for devils. If you habitually sin, more than likely there is a demon(s) involved. There is a distinct difference between a habit and a struggle. If you struggle with sin, then grace and mercy are your portion. If you make sinful behavior a habit, then you are literally inviting Satan to come in.

Do you remember the old Dracula movies? The title character was based on a real person called Vlad the Impaler. He was the second son of Vlad Dracul, who became the ruler of Wallachia in 1436.[4] The Ottoman sultan, Mehmed II, ordered Vlad to pay homage to him personally, but Vlad had the sultan's two envoys captured and impaled. In February 1462, he attacked Ottoman territory, massacring tens of thousands of Turks and Bulgarians.

As we can clearly see, his moniker was well earned. He was an evil king who terrorized others, even those he ruled, very much like Satan does today. The mythical Dracula was a vampire who could not come into someone's residence unless he was invited. Lucifer and his servants operate in the same manner. They cannot enter a human body unless they're asked in. They may obtain *permission* through ancestors, accidents, actions, personal sin, or direct request.

This is the reason why many find themselves in a worse state after the death of a demonically afflicted family member. They face a greater battle for deliverance because the demons come in and link up with the familiar spirits that already reside there. This causes them to be an even greater force for evil. The saying is true—there really is strength in numbers.

To combat such an army, we must be quick to recognize that the Greater One lives inside of those who are born again.

> *Ye are of God, little children, and have overcome them: because greater is he that is in you, than he that is in the world* (1 John 4:4).

How Do You Know If You're Free?

You know you're free from a particular demon when you no longer do its job. What I mean by this statement is that demons use the human body to express their depraved nature. They are incorporeal beings that require a body to express themselves. For example, they may cause a person to engage in homosexuality, fornication, drug use, murder, and other sins. Their primary occupation is to get you to do things that you know are wrong or sinful in the eyes of God. They can't make you do these things. Demons act upon the hidden desires that are already within the person.

When pinpointed, a relentless barrage of imagery is flooded, not just into the mind, but also into the soul. As the individual focuses upon the devilish images consistently, the process of its manifestation begins. Remember, we innately have a tendency to become our greatest thoughts. As mentioned before, we will eventually do that which we meditate on the longest. This is why the Scriptures are clear regarding what we should think about.

> *And now, dear brothers and sisters, one final thing.*
> *Fix your thoughts on what is true, and honorable, and*
> *right, and pure, and lovely, and admirable. Think*
> *about things that are excellent and worthy of praise*
> (Philippians 4:8, NLT).

When our thoughts are finally able to line up with the things listed in this verse, we know that we have overcome Satan, mentally. The enemy may send an evil thought or image past your mind, but the fruit of the spirit—self-control—is in place to prompt us to cast it down as we remain submitted to Christ. (See Second Corinthians 10:4-5.)

BE AUTHENTIC. BE WILLING. BE FREE.

Some of the greatest deliverance you can receive is not only from demons, but also *people*! To be free from the opinions, desires, and approval of others concerning your endeavors is one of the most liberating feelings in the entire world. Sadly, there are very few who have mastered this art. The more delivered you are from other individuals' thoughts, opinions, criticisms, and judgments, the more kingdom focused you will become. You can't let anything detour you from the mandate of God upon your life. We must all come to the realization that some people are demonically inspired to prevent you from being all you can be in Him. Essentially, demons don't want you to be great in God.

If you're serving the Lord to be liked or popular, then you're not really serving the Lord; you're using Him! In this season, God is pinpointing the authentic and raising them up. They are, even as I'm writing this, replacing the old guard. The old guard must be willing, like Elijah in relation to Elisha, to anoint and mantle their successors, even while they are still living. They must be like John in reference to Jesus, to whom he lost his entire congregation without a murmur, harsh word, or complaint.

If we can get delivered from the praise and the curses of men, then true freedom will be realized. The false will be discerned or distinguished from the true. Words will not be just given to placate, but they will also be used to impart and replicate authenticity.

When I say replicate authenticity, I'm referring to producing originals, not copies. I'm talking about being catalysts for independent thinkers, not just yes men, making disciples instead of armor-bearers. We have enough people in the church washing cars, holding jackets, carrying briefcases, and standing guard so that nobody will attack the leader while they're preaching. We've had enough of the lack of deliverance teams or presbyteries. We've had enough of a good "whoop" (entertaining style of preaching) without solid teaching and training, which is needed to equip saints for battle.

How many in the church can cast out a devil or engage in spiritual warfare? This question needs to be addressed and answered in every church that belongs to Jesus Christ.

Let's encourage free thought instead of charging for it. Let get real again! Let our speech be seasoned with salt instead of pepper. Let's allow our words to carry the weight of integrity. Let's truly be who we are called to be in Him. Let us be peculiar. Like Daniel, let's dare to be different!

Stop worrying about whether others acknowledge you or not! Don't get offended if they don't speak. Don't get mad if they don't share their pulpit or platform with you. Don't talk about them in secret then smile in their faces as if nothing is wrong.

Get delivered from the actions of others! Allow God to build His platform for you, instead of attempting to build it yourself. Remember, anything that's formed carnally will die! Today, God is raising up the least likely to succeed and bringing down those who, in their own eyes, are the most likely to succeed.

One of Satan's objectives is for us to be people pleasers. The constant pursuit of making others happy is truly an exercise in futility. It's impossible to do this with fidelity and consistency. No one should be a barometer for your success or failure. You should not allow others to live in your head rent-free! You evict them by allowing God to not only be your head, but also live in it as well.

> *For am I now seeking the approval of man, or of God?*
> *Or am I trying to please man? If I were still trying*
> *to please man, I would not be a servant of Christ*
> (Galatians 1:10, ESV).

When you have mastery over your own spirit and are not disrupted by men-pleasing spirits and other temptations or sinful behaviors, you can begin to step into the realm of deliverance ministry with faith and confidence.

WHEN YOU'RE CALLED TO DELIVERANCE MINISTRY

When Moses first threw down his rod under the instruction of God, it represented the casting off of his old identity. When it hit the ground, it turned into a snake and Moses fled from it. Sometimes the realization of who you are in God will cause you to flee. Many people today are running from their true identity, but it's time to come back to it. Moses returned and picked the snake up by the tail. It became a rod again, and Moses became a deliverer. That which scared him became the instrument God used to help deliver millions!

It's time to throw down who you thought you were and pick up who you're supposed to be in God. When you embrace the new identity you picked up, a new sound will emit from you. This is a sound that attracts God. This sound is even heard through your praise and worship.

Authentic praise is one of your greatest weapons against the enemy. He especially hates it when you're able to worship the Lord when he's unleashed all of hell against you. When it's combined with quality prayer, it's even more effective in putting devils on the run! As evidenced by Paul and Silas, prayer and praise can cause a shaking, which subsequently sets captives free. I believe that this can be applied to a demonically oppressed individual. The shaking will ultimately create pathways for liberation.

OUR FIRST DELIVERANCE SESSION

Heal the sick, cleanse the lepers, raise the dead, cast out devils: freely ye have received, freely give (Matthew 10:8).

When we first started our church, Enduring Faith Christian Center, in 2002, I had very limited exposure to actual deliverance sessions. The first time I was a part of such an event was at the ministry prior to starting my own. It occurred in 2000 during prayer for one of the members. Without warning, a foreign voice came out of this very soft-spoken male congregant, along with growls and snorts. He displayed superhuman strength, taking three large men, including myself, to hold him down. While on the ground, the demonized individual almost lifted us off of him! After coming against the demons that were obviously inside of him in Jesus's name, he reverted to a normal state, unable to recall the previous goings on.

I had never seen anything like this in the house of God. It was both alarming and intriguing at the same time. We later found out that this same person had been cheating on his wife for years. Adultery is a common avenue by which demons get in. This guy was so perverse that he subtly came on to my wife. I addressed him and his demons, but that's another story for another time.

In the early 2000s, on a cold fall Wednesday evening, our church, Enduring Faith Christian Center (www.faith2endure.com), was having its weekly prayer service. This particular meeting turned out to be a vast departure from what we'd been previously used to. In the midst of our prayers, a young lady started manifesting a demon. It shook us because we never had this happen in our ministry before. Several of us ran to her and began *shouting deliverance* at her. This was a mistake, based on being novices to this type of spiritual attack.

A voice spewed from this woman's mouth that didn't belong to her. It was deeper, and much more masculine. It said, "You can't cast me out because there's no power here!"

Though a bit shaken, we pressed on anyway. After a while, tranquility literally walked into the room and she settled down. We all know it was Jesus who came in. Know Jesus, know peace.

Even though she was calm and the alien voice subsided, I felt that we hadn't really done anything significant in terms of her deliverance. So, afterward, I consulted a good friend of mine who is a prophet and well-seasoned in the arena of casting out devils. I expressed our apparent failure and communicated my despondency. The response he gave was prophetic and relieving. He stated that we had done more damage to the kingdom of hell than we thought. We did? It sure didn't feel like it at the time, but that evening would prove otherwise.

When my wife and I arrived home that night, an eerie feeling circulated within the house. Though I wasn't sure, I perceived that it was a result of what happened earlier. While in my office, my wife, Elisa, frantically bolted in with a look of extreme concern on her face. She asked me to come to our bedroom. Elisa pointed out a horrifying image that has been indelibly etched into my mind ever since. It was an inverted cross formed out of a substance that looked like some type of tainted or dirty oil. Someone or *something* did this. During this time, we had no children or other people living with us; it was just my wife and me.

I immediately began to pray and rebuke the devil, while concurrently using a dampened washcloth to wipe off the blasphemous symbol. What the prophet told me earlier instantly came to mind—you were more effective than you thought.

The devil didn't stop there. The next night, I was attacked by something I couldn't see. While sleeping, I was jarred awake by a strong shot of pain that raced down my arm. I looked down at my right arm and could see the muscle in my forearm being squeezed repeatedly by an invisible hand! I came against this spirit with the name of Jesus! In a couple of minutes, it departed. To give further credence to this incident, upon waking the next day, there was a purplish bruise on my right forearm.

These attacks and others convinced me that Satan will not just stand by and let you attack his kingdom. We must always be on guard against retaliation that comes from taking the offensive against the dark forces. Like a worker bee that will sting you for assailing the hive it protects, demons will fervently defend their current habitation. When operating in deliverance, we must walk by faith and not by sight (see 2 Cor. 5:7). Sense or human knowledge may say that you've failed, but what did God say? Oftentimes, you're more successful than what your physical vision indicates. Remember, we see with the mind through the eyes. Satan will always attempt to blind the minds of those who believe, especially when it comes to supernatural deliverance.

> *In whom the god of this world hath blinded the minds of them which believe not, lest the light of the glorious gospel of Christ, who is the image of God, should shine unto them* (2 Corinthians 4:4).

As deliverance workers, we should pray for God to open our spiritual eyes to see Him at work and to see the forces of heaven on our side. May we see what Elisha saw:

> *And he answered, Fear not: for they that be with us are more than they that be with them.*
>
> *And Elisha prayed, and said, Lord, I pray thee, open his eyes, that he may see. And the Lord opened the eyes of the young man; and he saw: and, behold, the mountain was full of horses and chariots of fire round about Elisha* (2 Kings 6:16-17).

There are more for us than against us. With God, we always win the battle against darkness.

CHAPTER 11

DELIVERANCE 101:
DON'T TALK TO STRANGERS

They [sheep] won't follow a stranger; they will run from him because they don't know his voice.
—JOHN 10:5, NLT

As formerly stated, I have widely held the view that it is unwise to have an ongoing dialogue with demons. One reason being, like their father, Satan, they're prone to lie.

> *Ye are of your father the devil, and the lusts of your father ye will do. He was a murderer from the beginning, and abode not in the truth, because there is no truth in him. When he speaketh a lie, he speaketh of his own: for he is a liar, and the father of it* (John 8:44).

From the verse above, we see that the truth does not abide in Satan, so we can reasonably assume that truth doesn't dwell within his servants (demons) either. How can you count on the words of a devil when you know that honesty has no place in him? The more you converse with the dark angels of the enemy, the more confused you will become. The devil is the author (originator, creator, and architect) of confusion. Wherever there are confused people, Satan is nearby. He lives on and in confusion because the Lord didn't originate it.

> *For God is not the author of confusion, but of peace,*
> *as in all churches of the saints* (1 Corinthians 14:33).

If God didn't initiate confusion, then He's not in it. The Lord makes His home inside that which voluntarily opens itself up to Him. Everything good that was made by Him suits or fits Him. In fact, the great things that are made by God are *worn* by Him.

In Genesis 2:7, we read that the Lord breathed His Spirit (*pneuma*) into the nostrils of the man. He formed him from dust and man became a living soul. The word *pneuma* is Greek and means wind, breath, or spirit. God's Spirit or breath lives inside of each of us. While we are children of the Most High by choice, we are all His creation because of the gift of the breath of life. If His wind is in me, then I'm a part of Him, and He me. In other words, we are all the Lord's creation, but everyone is not a son or daughter of His. We become children of God when we accept Jesus Christ as our Lord and Savior. My position is based on what I've read in Scripture, experience and observation.

WHAT DOES THE BIBLE SAY ABOUT TALKING TO DEMONS?

The verses below give credence to the long-held belief and warning that you shouldn't talk to strangers. The devil and his crew are strangers to the Christian. I'm not saying that we should not be aware of their tactics. Great military leaders of the past have adhered to the fact that we should know our enemies and their strategies. This doesn't necessarily mean that we have to be taken in by their lies. We only need to extract the information needed to win the war.

There is a distinct reason behind a mother's intuition when cautioning their children not to speak to people they're unfamiliar with. She is primarily concerned about their safety. As a mother, she intuitively knows the danger that may lurk behind the beguiling smile of a stranger. Well, so does God, yet even more so!

> *And in the synagogue there was a man, which had a spirit of an unclean devil, and cried out with a loud voice, saying, Let us alone; what have we to do with thee, thou Jesus of Nazareth? art thou come to destroy us? I know thee who thou art; the Holy One of God. And Jesus rebuked him, saying, Hold thy peace, and come out of him. And when the devil had thrown him in the midst, he came out of him, and hurt him not* (Luke 4:33-35).

In the Aramaic Bible in Plain English, Luke 4:35 reads as follows:

> *And Yeshua rebuked it and he said, "Shut your mouth and come out of him!" And the demon threw him in the midst, and it came out from him, while it did him no harm.*

In the Amplified Bible, the same verse says:

> *But Jesus rebuked him, saying, "Be silent (muzzled, gagged), and come out of him!"*

It's clearly evident, considering the verses above, that the Lord saw no purpose or value in hearing what demons had to say. Jesus told Satan to shut up and come out, and so should we.

They want you to keep talking.

As mentioned before, the longer you talk to them while in a deliverance session, the longer they will stay! They remain to listen, engage, and distract the deliverance worker. In other words, demons want you to keep the conversation going. They want you to ask them questions to your heart's content. The more you do, the more time they have to establish their lies in you. Once the lies are planted in you, they have a tendency to grow into false truths.

Remember the lies the serpent told Eve in the third chapter of Genesis? Satan first appealed to her curiosity in reference to what she couldn't have. He then moved on to a one-on-one conversation so that he could establish his lies. The snake did this by mixing falsehoods with biblical truth.

> *Now the serpent was more subtil than any beast of the field which the Lord God had made. And he said unto the woman, Yea, hath God said, Ye shall not eat of every tree of the garden?*
>
> *And the woman said unto the serpent, We may eat of the fruit of the trees of the garden: but of the fruit of the tree which is in the midst of the garden, God hath said, Ye shall not eat of it, neither shall ye touch it, lest ye die.*
>
> *And the serpent said unto the woman, Ye shall not surely die: For God doth know that in the day ye eat*

thereof, then your eyes shall be opened, and ye shall be as gods, knowing good and evil.

And when the woman saw that the tree was good for food, and that it was pleasant to the eyes, and a tree to be desired to make one wise, she took of the fruit thereof, and did eat, and gave also unto her husband with her; and he did eat (Genesis 3:1-6).

They are conversation starters.

Notice in the above verses, the serpent initiated the conversation. Oftentimes, the devil will begin speaking to you before you realize that it's him. This has happened to me many times, especially in my younger years. I would often mistake Satan's voice for God's, and it would place me in dire situations. Please realize that the devil will frequently mimic the voice of God to fool you into thinking that it's Him speaking to you.

Be sober, be vigilant; because your adversary the devil, as a roaring lion, walketh about, seeking whom he may devour (1 Peter 5:8).

You need to know God's voice.

Satan may go around mimicking the sound of the Lion of Judah, but you and I know that is not who he is. As previously mentioned, we must always be able to differentiate His sound (voice) from that of a stranger (the enemy). This is done through *koinonia* (Greek word for fellowship) with God. The more time we spend listening to His voice (sound), the more familiar with it we will become. The more we are able to identify His sound, the less likely that we will mistake it for Satan's sound.

Look who's talking to you! In other words, discern (see) the various voices that compete for your attention. The four main voices that vie for your consideration are: God's, your own, other people's and the devil's. It should be your goal to identify every sound that attempts to enter your ear gates.

> *The hearing ear and the seeing eye, the Lord has made them both* (Proverbs 20:12, ESV).

Don't answer the enemy.

In Genesis 3:1, the snake asked Eve a question to initiate the dialogue. When the enemy makes an inquiry of you, don't answer him. The answer is always linked to your future downfall in some way. It's evident here that the fate of humanity rested upon the results of this exchange. As soon as Eve answered, she revealed a secret longing within her heart—to eat of the tree that the Lord had strictly forbidden her to partake of.

As children, doing things that our parents told us not to do can be captivating. Please don't tell me that you resisted every time your mother or father asked you not to do something. I know I didn't!

> *Stolen water is sweet, and food eaten in secret tastes the best!* (Proverbs 9:17, NLT).

Honestly, when I was living in and with sin, it was fun. Why? Because my mind hadn't been renewed in Christ yet. The whimsical nature of doing things we should not do appeals to our flesh, but repulses our spirits. Our spirits consistently desire to do that which is right in the eyes of the Lord. The body, on the other hand, does not.

An illustration of this is found in the simple act of getting up for work in the morning—our spirits are ready to go, but numerous times our flesh is not. It has a tendency to hit the snooze button multiple times before finally getting up.

One thing that we must realize is that our spirits never sleep. They are always waiting, willing, and able, but sometimes our flesh overrides our spirits. Remember, whatever you feed the most will dominate you. If you allow your body to rule you, then the result will be weakness. If you allow your spirit to be sovereign over your body, then you will begin to operate in power.

> *Keep watch and pray, so that you will not give in to temptation. For the spirit is willing, but the body is weak!* (Matthew 26:41, NLT).

Pray to fortify your spirit and body for war.

Whenever you're not walking with a circumspective perspective, you are likely to give in to enticements when your walk is not coupled with prayer. *Prayer fortifies the spirit and strengthens the body for war.*

Sometimes your spiritual battles are won on your knees, and not your feet. There are epochs (periods of time) when personal wars with the enemy are lost because we were standing when we should have been in a posture of genuflection (kneeling).

Satan uses conversation to uncover secret desires.

Everything the serpent said to Eve was a petition to her basic nature. Satan's strategy was to target that which he knew was in her based upon observation. Adam's wife was literally bound by what she secretly desired and so are many of us. When we first receive the astounding gift of salvation through Jesus Christ, some things that held us in bondage immediately dropped off. But there are others that linger because of the strength that was built up over time due to consistently giving in to temptation.

The Bible doesn't tell us how long Eve lived in the Garden of Eden. Adam and Eve could have lived there for thousands of years. In Genesis 4, after they were kicked out of the garden, Adam and Eve bore Cain and Abel. As mentioned previously in this book, Cain slew Abel because he gave God a more excellent offering than he did. As punishment, God cursed Cain and marked him, so that no man would kill him. Cain ventured out and lived in the land of Nod. He met his wife there and raised a family. Question: where did Cain's wife come from? Who birthed her? We only know that Adam and Eve had two children at this time. This leads me to believe that maybe there was another way or method of conceiving while they were in the Garden of Eden.

In Genesis 3:16, God told Eve that He would make her pains in child bearing very severe: "with painful labor you will give birth to children" (NIV). In my estimation, Eve must have had something to compare this to for God to say that she would have discomfort when birthing babies. My hypothesis is that she had other children pain-free, and they populated the land. Take into account that when God made them, he mandated that they be fruitful and multiply in order to replenish the earth.

> *And God blessed them, and God said unto them, **Be fruitful, and multiply, and replenish the earth,** and subdue it: and have dominion over the fish of the sea, and over the fowl of the air, and over every living*

thing that moveth upon the earth (Genesis 1:28, emphasis added).

Replenish means "to fill or build up again."[1] This made me wonder: what was here before that needed to be filled or built up again? The Lord instructed Adam and Eve to do this before the Fall, so would it be too far of a stretch to entertain the fact that Eve could have given birth to children while yet in the Garden of Eden?

Each of the two times in Scripture that the earth was just about void of life, the Lord instructed the people who remained to be fruitful, multiply, and replenish (to fill or build again) the earth. He did it with the first man and woman. God did the same thing with Noah and his sons after the great flood.

> *And God blessed Noah and his sons, and said unto them, Be fruitful, and multiply, and replenish the earth* (Genesis 9:1).

I hope that you get the gist of what I'm trying convey here. This mode of thinking began with my revelation of the conversation between a snake and a woman. I started to look behind the words and uncover their motivation. The serpent played upon Eve's desires—desires that motivate most people: the lust of the flesh, the lust of the eyes, and the pride of life. These three things cause people to be bound by Satan.

> *For all that is in the world, the lust of the flesh, and the lust of the eyes, and the pride of life, is not of the Father, but is of the world* (1 John 2:16).

All the elements found in First John 2:16 are evident in the Genesis 3:6, so it bears revisiting:

And when the woman saw that the tree was good for food [lust of the flesh], *and that it was pleasant to the eyes* [lust of the eyes] *and a tree to be desired to make one wise* [the pride of life], *she took the fruit thereof, and did eat, and gave also unto her husband with her, and he did eat.*

This miscalculation of judgment all began with talking to a stranger.

A Master Communicator and Manipulator

Is it wise to talk to devils? Not at all. I think we've established that point within the previous chapters at this juncture. Listening and responding to the snake (Satan) got Adam and Eve kicked out of the Garden of Eden (see Gen. 3). A tragic mistake that reverberates to this very day. We're all paying for Eve's dialogue with Satan now. Thanks, guys!

Satan is a master communicator and manipulator. He is the prince of the power of the air. Words travel on air. This gives Lucifer the ability to influence the air to affect words. He uses air to distort words, which, in turn, pervert truth. He literally uses truth as a *temporary* foundation for his lies. It's temporary because there is no truth in him. He only *uses truth* to establish his falsehoods. Satan constructs his lies on the pretense of honesty, but he refuses to let truth pervade that which he's endeavoring to build. This is because he's simply *prostituting truth* to give credibility to his lies in order to get you to believe them. The words are really falsehoods dressed up as veracity (truth).

Wherein in time past ye walked according to the course of this world, according to the prince of the power of the air, the spirit that now worketh in the children of disobedience (Ephesians 2:2).

Demons are spiritually dead; don't talk to the dead.

Demons are strangers to Christians. They are not familiar to them in the familial sense. We are to have no meaningful interaction with them beyond casting them out. Demons, to me, don't have life. They are essentially dead to God. There is no plan of redemption for the devil or his angels. They can never make heaven their home because it's a place for the eternally living not the eternally dead. In Scripture, we are warned not to consult the dead (necromancy).

And when they shall say unto you, Seek unto them that have familiar spirits, and unto wizards that peep, and that mutter: should not a people seek unto their God? for the living to the dead? (Isaiah 8:19).

You don't know him, so don't follow him.

In the parable of the Good Shepherd and His sheep, Jesus cautioned us not to follow the voice of those we don't know. There must be intimacy before following anyone. The ensuing verse was cited at the beginning of this chapter, but I'd like to revisit it here for further emphasis.

They [His sheep] won't follow a stranger; they will run from him because they don't know his voice (John 10:5, NLT).

You can ask for a name.

As stated in an earlier chapter, there was only one recorded occasion when Jesus asked a demon its name. He did this because the demon refused to go. If your father called you by name, would you answer? I would because, as my parent, my dad has authority over me. Jesus is our Father (see John 10:30—He and the Father are one), and though demons are employed by Satan, they cannot hurt a child of God unless the Lord gives them permission. In Job's case, *ole slew foot* (the devil) could not touch him until Jehovah gave him permission to do so (see Job 1:1-12).

Remember, it's okay to get a demon's name, but it's not wise to hold an extended conversation with them.

WHAT NOT TO ASK A DEMON

1. What do you know about the spirit realm?

2. What area of hell did you come from?

3. What about the demons in Mexico?

4. Who will I marry?

5. When will I die?

I think you catch my drift here. Again, demons will use the truth as an attempt to validate deceptive responses. Don't ever trust them. It will only lead to ruin. Sadly, some deliverance workers seem more interested in talking with demons than casting them out.

CUT THE CONVERSATION, AND JUST CAST THEM OUT!

Deliverance sessions should not take all night. In John 14:12, Jesus said, "Verily, verily, I say unto you, He that believeth on me, the works that I do shall he do also; and greater works than these shall he do; because I go unto my Father."

If He was able to cast out devils, then so should His sheep. All you have to do is believe on Him, and you will be able to do what He did and even greater!

This bears repeating here: extended conversations with devils inside a person actually prolong deliverance. Simply take your God-given authority over evil spirits and tell them to go!

My late spiritual mother, author Ruth Brown, taught me not to be overly concerned with calling out each demon in a person by name. She advised me to go after the strong man—the head devil in charge. Once he was cast out, the lower-ranking demons would go with him.

This revelation made so much sense to me. I'd seen poor souls demonized for years because deliverance workers sought to expel them all, individually, by name. My thought? What if a person had a thousand devils in them? Can you imagine how long that would take? A lifetime. I will elaborate more on the "strong man" in Chapter 12.

Do just as Jesus did with the young man who had demons in him called Legion.

But when he saw Jesus afar off, he ran and worshiped him, and cried with a loud voice, and said, What have I to do with you, Jesus, you Son of the most high God? I adjure you by God, that you torment me not.

For he had said unto him, Come out of the man, you unclean spirit.

And he asked him, What is your name? And he answered, saying, My name is Legion: for we are many (Mark 5:6-9).

Jesus ordered the demons to come out and asked only one question of the strong man or head demon. He secured what was needed to identify what inhabited the young man, then used it to cast out Legion (all of them). He didn't engage in casual conversation with them. He cast them out!

When someone asks you, "Do you think you can cast out a demon?"

You say, "In the name of Jesus, I know I can."

Remember, Lucifer doesn't want to be driven out of people. He will do his best to cast a spirit of doubt into you, so that you won't access your authority as a believer. He does this often. I've heard people give all kinds of excuses when it comes down to actually exorcising demons out of others. This is why one of my rules for victory over Satan, the father of lies, is "don't talk to strangers." If you want consistent victory and to keep your mind from falling prey to his deceptions, you will adopt this rule as well.

CHAPTER 12

HEALING, DELIVERANCE, AND THE PROPHETIC

That evening many demon-possessed people were
brought to Jesus. He cast out the evil spirits with
a simple command, and he healed all the sick.
—MATTHEW 8:16, NLT

In the verse above, Jesus cast out devils before He healed the sick. In many cases, demons are the culprits behind infirmity. They can be the main obstacle to you walking in divine health. It's their goal to hold you within the clutches of illness in an attempt to commandeer the healing that the Lord has promised you in Scripture.

As of the date of this writing, there has been an increase in teachings and demonstrations in reference to healing in the church. I believe that this is due to God's strong desire to heal in this hour. The Lord's nature or heart is to heal nouns (people, places, and things). The wonderful thing about Him is that He doesn't change. It's still His will to heal you! Healing is something that belongs to you. It's your divine right to expect wholeness in every area of your life! Why shouldn't you? He is the Lord that heals thee (Jehovah Rapha). In order to be whole, you have to be supernaturally delivered!

> *When Jesus saw him lie, and knew that he had been now a long time in that case, he saith unto him, Wilt thou be made whole?* (John 5:6).

When Jesus saw him and knew he had been ill for a long time, He asked him, "Would you like to get well?" In another version of the Bible, Jesus asks, "Do you want to be healed?" This is the same question Jesus is asking us today: Will you be made whole?

DIVINE WHOLENESS

God's initial plan for man was for us to be like Him—whole, lacking absolutely nothing! This is the reason that He made us in His image and likeness. I believe that He still desires that for us today.

> *Then God said, "Let us make human beings in our image, to be like us. They will reign over the fish in the sea, the birds in the sky, the livestock, all the wild animals on the earth, and the small animals that scurry along the ground"* (Genesis 1:26, NLT).

The definition of *wholeness* according to the *Merriam-Webster Dictionary* is "The condition of being sound in body. The quality or state of being without restriction, exception, or qualification."[1] Its antonyms include *imperfection, unsoundness,* etc.[2] Notice that the word *imperfection* is an antonym for *wholeness*, which leads me to believe that perfection should be its synonym. In essence, wholeness equals perfection!

*And they were both naked, the man and his wife, and
were not ashamed* (Genesis 2:25).

Adam and Eve lived in a state of perpetual perfection or
wholeness. Shame, embarrassment, and fear were foreign to them.
It wasn't until their act of disobedience that these *"spirits"* were
factors for them. As long as we heed the instructions of the Most
High, wholeness will be who we are. Why? Because the Holy Spirit
is whole and dwells in every believer.

When you are supernaturally delivered, perfection is yours to
claim. Many will purport that this is impossible, but the Bible says
nothing is impossible for God (see Luke 1:37, CEV). When you're
whole, the spirit of shame has no place in you. When you're whole,
fear can't live in you. When you're whole, the spirit of embarrassment will not be your portion.

HOW TO STAY WHOLE

In order to stay whole (healed), you must listen to and follow the
directives of God. What He says may seem to go against conventional wisdom, but we have to do as the Lord instructs. Do you
want to walk in supernatural healing? Listen to God.

Many stay sick due to listening to the devil or people over God.
For example, the enemy will tell you that you will be bound to
medication your entire life when God is saying, "Not so!" There is
nothing that the Lord wants you to be enslaved to, including medication. Satan's will is for you to be in everlasting bondage to things
that will eventually destroy you!

Each utterance that proceeds out of the devil's mouth is
designed to kill, steal from you, and in the end, destroy you. If you

can attune your spiritual ears to His voice, it will drown out the words of the evil one. As you adhere to His voice and follow His commands, your healing will spring forth speedily!

In this dispensation, there will be an increase in believers who are facing life-threatening diseases being miraculously healed by the power of the Holy Spirit. Even after being cured, the Lord will *download* instructions for staying healed. Illnesses can and will return if we don't heed the wisdom, warnings, and counsel of God. When Jesus healed the impotent man at the pool of Bethesda, He warned him about continuing to do things God did not approve of.

> *After these things Jesus finds him in the temple, and said to him, Behold, thou art become well: sin no more, that something worse do not happen to thee.*
> *The man went away and told the Jews that it was Jesus who had made him well* (John 5:14-15, Darby).

Though the impotent man relied on men to get healed, he learned that it had to come from Jesus. Your dependence should not be placed solely on others, but the Lord. I believe that it's a sin to place all your confidence in men. Sin opens the door to worse things happening. There are persons whom the Lord will tell to change their diet, start an exercise program, rest, or lower their stress levels. In some cases, they don't heed His directives and end up in a worse state. This is the hour to do what the Lord instructs in order to maintain your wholeness.

I literally see healing revivals breaking out all over the country, in which many will be delivered from all manner of sickness. The oil of healing has saturated the atmosphere. Those who truly hear the heart of God will echo this sentiment. Books will be written on the subject of healing during this time period. Leaders will feel led to minister on, write about, and elaborate on the subject. In return, they will see healing manifest within their own ministries.

Don't Ask for It–Decree It!

Very often, we're not healed because we ask for it instead of decreeing it by faith. Yes, you heard me correctly. A great number of healings in Scripture were received by people who made statements based in faith instead of asking questions.

For example, the woman with the issue of blood in Matthew 9:21 said within herself, "If I may but touch His garment, I shall be whole." Once she made this statement and touched Jesus's robe, her faith made her whole!

Notice that Jesus didn't intentionally heal her; her faith did. Her decree had faith as its foundation. That faith caused her to move. Her touch pulled virtue (power) out of our Lord and she was made whole!

The centurion soldier said, in Matthew 8:8, "Lord, I am not worthy that thou shouldest come under my roof: but speak the word only, and my servant shall be healed." He made a statement and his servant was healed in that selfsame hour!

In some cases, Jesus was the one asking the infirmed questions, putting them in position to make statements in relation to their health. Stop asking to be healed and start decreeing it! If you decree a thing, it will be established (see Job 22:28).

GET DELIVERED AND BE HEALED

Remember, the wicked one is behind most illnesses. Deliverance is key in being set free from them. Even after receiving good health, we must maintain it. That entails adhering to the counsel or instruction of the Most High. If this occurs, sustained healing will be achieved.

I see people not only getting physically healed, but emotionally and mentally as well. Revival will come in the midst of our praise. In fact, I see people actually getting healed during anointed praise and worship. As long as the fire of revival blazes, we will see signs, wonders, and miracles. There will be numerous people who will testify that it was the Lord who healed them of cancer, heart disease, AIDS, diabetes, and a host of demonic ailments. Many will experience deliverance from evil spirits, which will result in sicknesses being automatically evacuated from their bodies.

The enemy usually tries to stricken the body so that we're unable to function in our duties toward Christ. Throughout the New Testament, there were cases in which demons attacked the victim's health. Sickness and deliverance are mutually exclusive. When there's one, the other is not far behind. Some stay in their conditions due to not receiving proper and balanced deliverance ministry.

> *But this kind of demon does not go out except by prayer and fasting* (Matthew 17:21, AMP).

This verse applies to the spirit of infirmity as well. Evil spirits can be cast out, but some are stronger than others. Times of prayer and fasting are needed in order to deal with these high-ranking entities. When this happens, healing and deliverance are the primary outcomes.

PROPHETIC DELIVERANCE

No man can enter into a strong man's house, and spoil his goods, except he will first bind the strong man; and then he will spoil his house (Mark 3:27).

There is such a thing as prophetic deliverance. I've honestly never read or heard of anyone using this term. It's a revelation I received from the Lord while actively engaged in the ministry of casting out devils. Prophetic deliverance is simply using the gift of prophecy (mainly words of knowledge), in unity with the gift of discernment, to identify specific satanic strongholds, name them, and cast them out.

I'm of the mindset that prophetic ministry and deliverance go hand in hand. It's very common to see both forms of ministry evident within true apostolic houses. To see one without the other is concerning. God will usually speak to you or provide a word of knowledge while or before casting out devils.

The prophetic gift is crucial to deliverance. In my estimation, the best people to cast out demons are those who have a sturdy prophetic dimension. As a prophet, I've noticed that my aptitude to see in the spirit realm has aided me in detecting demons that have become embedded within individuals. Once I've perceived their presence in the spirit realm, I'm able to call them out, in the name of Jesus Christ, in the natural realm.

As you probably know by now, I do not recommend engaging in conversation with devils, but identifying them within an individual is imperative to casting them out, as in the case of dealing with the strongman (a.k.a., chief or head demon), lightly addressed in Chapter 11, that lies within. There is a hierarchy within the kingdom of Satan. It's very similar to a natural army. There are generals, captains, sergeants, corporals, and the like.

Identifying the Strongman

In reference to the scripture at the beginning of this section, how can we know who the strongman is? We can know through the prophetic DNA (ability to hear God's voice) that exists in every believer. Once identified, as touched upon earlier, a deliverance worker can bind him up and cast the strongman out of a demonized person. The weaker or lower-ranking demons will exit with him. In medieval times, when the king or most powerful warrior (e.g. Goliath) was defeated, it left the soldiers scattered and fearful, making them easier to kill or capture.

I'm in total agreement with this philosophy. I see casting out the chief devil as a catalyst that ignites a literal and spiritual chain reaction. Each of the lower-level or weaker demons are *chained* to the most powerful one. When he's thrown out of the house (our bodies), the others go because they're linked to him. It's similar to a heavy ball with a chain attached, being thrown off a bridge and into the water. Whatever is attached to that chain that weighs less than the ball will be pulled in.

You have to get rid of what is demonically weightier in the spirit to get to the demons that are lighter, spiritually. As touched upon in Chapter 11, if you only go after the minor-league demons, total freedom or eviction of the spirits in the sufferer may take years. Again, this may be contrary to conventional thinking regarding deliverance, but calling out all the names of lesser demons is counterproductive. It simply wastes valuable time, especially if the person receiving deliverance has hundreds or even thousands of devils that have made his or her body their home. Why not use the gift of discernment or a word of knowledge (a component of prophecy) to identify the general (head demon) within and cast him out? If this is done, his foot soldiers will follow. I call this *efficient deliverance*.

EFFICIENT DELIVERANCE

The word *efficient* means "performing or functioning in the best possible manner with the least waste of time and effort."[3] This type of deliverance should be practiced by all ministers of deliverance. The competency and success rate of casting out devils would surely increase. You're cutting out the middle man and going straight for the source.

Your goal is to rid the demonized person of the chief evil spirit, but he must first be bound (incapacitated). You do this by invoking the powerful name of Jesus Christ, calling the spirit by name, and binding him. Once constrained, the demon is rendered powerless over the individual and is more easily evicted.

After restraining him, you're able to spoil his house (body). Whenever demons enter a body, they refer to it as their place of dwelling. Spoiling his house entails getting rid of all of the strongman's imps. Remember, where he goes, they go! He leaves, they go with him. Doesn't this sound like efficient deliverance? It does to me too.

In conclusion, the prophetic is very important in supernatural deliverance. It's efficient and time-saving in terms of getting people supernaturally delivered.

CONCLUSION

PROTECT YOUR OIL

*And it shall come to pass in that day, that his
burden shall be taken away from off thy shoulder,
and his yoke from off thy neck, and the yoke shall
be destroyed because of the anointing* [fatness].
—Isaiah 10:27

We've come to the end of this part of the journey to being supernaturally delivered. The whole of it never ends as we are always being perfected in Christ until the day we are changed from mortal to immortal and corruptible to incorruptible (see 1 Cor. 15:53-55). You have bravely shared in the many strange and otherworldly encounters my family and I have experienced. I pray you have come out with a greater sense of your power over the enemy and an increased desire to walk in divine discernment, so that he will not continue to invade your life.

At this point, you've learned about how the enemy comes in, your role in removing his presence, getting supernaturally delivered, and how to set others free. Now I want to show you how you can maintain your deliverance and protect the oil of anointing that has been given to you by the Holy Spirit.

Judges 16 tells the story of Samson and Delilah (please read this chapter as a reference for this treatise), which contains the revelation I received regarding the seven secrets to guarding your anointing. I earnestly believe that these secrets will help preserve the strength, vision, and effectiveness of your own God-given oil. It will assist you in avoiding the pitfalls Samson—and many others like him—fell into.

GUARDED AT ALL COSTS

In using Samson's life lesson, we discover that the anointing upon one's life must be guarded at all costs. Satan desires to know the secret of your effectiveness in the Lord so that he can keep you imprisoned. Just as there is a cost for the oil, there is also a payment due when its secrets are revealed before the appropriate time.

The oil that was on Samson is referred to in Judges 14:6 as "the Spirit of the Lord" being upon him when performing great feats of strength or leaving him when his hair was cut. This shows that the anointing can come and go. During this period of time, the Spirit of the Lord came and went as well. Wherever the Spirit of the Lord is, the oil has a tendency to flow. Saul is another prime example of this.

In First Samuel 15, Saul lost the kingdom due to disobeying God, but it doesn't state that the anointing was lost in Scripture. The kingdom referred to Saul's throne, while the anointing dealt with his effectiveness within the will of the Lord.

Some people erroneously believe that they are always anointed. Again, I'm referring to effectiveness. I disagree that we are always and consistently effective (anointed) in the Spirit.

Though God had left the king, His Spirit still dwelt in Israel. Where the Lord's Spirit lives, so will His anointing. I personally believe that the godly oil that was on King Saul when he was in His will lifted after the Lord left him. Though the king was no longer anointed, Israel still was.

FATTER IN THE SPIRIT

Isaiah 10:27 clearly states that when the anointing is present, burdens are removed and yokes are destroyed. If this isn't happening, then that person, place, or thing was not highly anointed of God at that particular moment. Some versions of the Bible use the words *fat, fatness*, or *prosperity* as other translations for the word *anointing*.

> *On that day the burden will be lifted from your shoulders, and the yoke from your neck. The yoke will be broken because of your fatness* (Isaiah 10:27, BSB).

This verse is referencing how the yoked animal's neck becomes so fat or enlarged that it destroys the yoke (that which holds it captive). Likewise, when your anointing increases, so does your fatness and prosperity. Being fatter in the spirit will cause you to have victory in the natural. In fact, Samson was so anointed that, in Judges chapter 15, he had the supernatural strength to kill one thousand men with the fresh jawbone of a donkey!

How the Anointing Works

The Spirit of the Lord is the anointing of God. According to *Merriam-Webster Dictionary*, the word *anoint* means "to smear or rub with oil."[1] Oil essentially represents the anointing, and the words are often used interchangeably in Scripture and other Christian discourse.

In biblical times, oil was poured upon the heads of sheep to prevent insects from attacking. They would set up camp around or on the head, then migrate to places around its ears and/or nostrils. Once in, these insects (lice and ticks) burrow deep into the sheep's brain, killing it over time. In response to this, shepherds would pour a substance, commonly a mixture of olive oil, on the top of the sheep's head. It would eventually run down its ears making them too slippery for the bugs to cling on to.[2]

As it was for sheep in the natural, so should it be that the spiritual oil upon your life covers you to the point that whenever demons try to latch on to you, they slip off!

It always begins at the top.

Notice that the oil was poured on the sheep's head. The anointing always begins at the top (head) and flows down as Psalm 133:2 alludes to with Israel's high priest, Aaron:

> *It is like precious oil poured on the head, running down on the beard, running down on Aaron's beard, down on the collar of his robe* (NIV).

The devil's first target is always the head (your mind). If he's able to infiltrate the brain, he can secure the body. This is the reason that our thoughts should be covered (concealed) and not always revealed. Some people say that the devil cannot read our minds. In my studies, I've never encountered any Scripture to support this theory. They assume he doesn't know what's going on in our brains. To be on the safe side, we must actively guard our thought lives. We can accomplish this by meditating on the things the Lord commands us to.

> *And now, dear brothers and sisters, one final thing.*
> *Fix your thoughts on what is true, and honorable, and*
> *right, and pure, and lovely, and admirable. Think*
> *about things that are excellent and worthy of praise*
> (Philippians 4:8, NLT).

The secret to Samson's strength was closely guarded information because if it fell into the wrong hands it would mean his utter defeat. We should do likewise in relation to ourselves. As with Jesus Christ, there are times when we are required to refrain from divulging the source of our breakthroughs, miracles, and the oil upon our lives.

Conceal the oil until the appointed time.

Jesus used parables to conceal His original messages for those who couldn't handle the truth. The anointing we may or may not carry comes directly from the Lord. He is the giver of the oil. This oil is specific to each of us, none being identical to the other. One may require an anointing for breakthrough, another for healing, and another for revival. Every anointing has a precise purpose and function.

Satan is not omniscient (all-knowing) like God. Therefore, Satan is not privy to all the Lord knows. There are some things about you the Lord will not allow Satan to see. In some cases, it could be the oil that's upon your life.

The enemy may have witnessed the anointing for a millennium, but God has a fresh, new anointing for each proceeding generation of believers. The devil is unable to accurately predict every new wave of the Spirit. He may assume, but he doesn't always know with assurance. The enemy may get a revelation of the oil, but it's usually after its utilization. As it says in Ecclesiastes 3:1, there is a season (period of time) for everything, even the revelation that makes its home within the anointing.

The oil is the key to unlocking various royal domains in the kingdom.

For every realm (royal domain or kingdom), there is a revelation. In order to receive it, you must live in the kingdom and not outside it. There are royal domains in the spirit for which certain types of oil are specifically designed. Royal domains include, but are not limited to, revelations regarding healing, deliverance, prophecy, discernment, and so on. Access is being granted due to the oil on our lives that comes from the daily trials and tribulations germane to citizens of the kingdom. Enduring hardness as a good soldier of Jesus Christ increases not only your anointing, but also your chance for admission to royal domains. By entering this domain, there will be a realization of your effectiveness as it relates to your kingdom assignment from God. The oil is the proverbial key to that certain area of the kingdom.

Our anointing gives us access, but our spoken words can delay or deny entry. Sometimes we divulge things the Lord didn't want us to say. It may be the wrong time or season to speak it. When

"*Delilahs*" (people who disclose your confidences in order to harm you) obtain the secret to your anointing, they may reveal it to your enemy. Once they know its architecture or structure, they're armed with information on how to deny access.

James 5:16 instructs us to confess our faults to one another, but that doesn't include exposing the secrets of our effectiveness (oil). I'm in no way saying that you're not to share information that will assist others in heading in the direction of their destinies. I am saying that you must prayerfully consider whom you are sharing the infrastructure or inner workings of your anointing with. For instance, does your effectiveness increase when you pray or in a powerful prayer-filled environment? Does your anointing begin to flow when there are strong gifts of prophecy at work or when people are getting delivered? If you know the environment or atmosphere in which your oil starts to flow, you must be careful and prayerful about revealing this to people who are being used by Satan. If the enemy gets a hold of this information, he'll do everything in his power to stop it.

In the case of Samson, he revealed his secret to the wrong person. It led to his ineffectiveness and demise.

God has not called you tell everybody everything about your life. There are people who lie in wait just to capture your conversations and compile them together, in order to find out things you haven't openly shared. These individuals are really representatives sent by the enemy to discover just what propels your effectiveness. Once discovered, demonic strategies are devised to try to stop the mandate of God upon your life from being fulfilled.

With Samson, he used Delilah. What or whom will he use with you?

Sin taints the oil.

A common theme in Samson's life was a weakness for women. Just before he was so in love with Delilah, he was with a prostitute. The devil loves to taint your oil! There are many who start with a fresh, clear anointing, but it can become stale and cloudy due to spiritual stains that build up over time. Spiritual stains result from our having ties to people, places, or things (nouns) that God does not approve of. Sin taints the anointing.

When the enemy discovers the secret of your oil, plans to set you up immediately follow, like that unexpected phone call from an old boyfriend or girlfriend. As previously stated, the adversary of our souls doesn't have any new tricks. He just brings back that which once held you in bondage. If women or men were your weakness in the past, he's not coming at you with alcohol!

Daniel 7:25 lets us know that the enemy's job is to oppress us and wear us out. This is how he used Delilah when it came to Sampson. She continually badgered Samson about the secret of his anointing to the point that, out of exhaustion, he told her. Judges 16:16 stated that Samson was "vexed unto death"! Delilah came to Samson several times with the same request, and each time he told her a fabricated story. In answer to each lie, Delilah attempted to have him captured by his enemies. The only reason it didn't succeed was because Samson wasn't honest with her. Just because it's the truth doesn't necessarily mean that it should always be revealed. I'm not advocating lying, but there were situations in which Jesus instructed formerly ill people not to tell others about their healing. Yes, it was the truth, but it wasn't time for it to be told.

Wrong association makes the oil vulnerable.

Here's another perspective to consider: the company we keep. True friends and covenant partners are not sly and out to sabotage us. Delilah revealed her mission several times over, but Samson stayed in her company. It's not so much about whether you conceal the truth, avoiding being honest. It's about fleeing the scene, as Joseph did in response to unwanted sexual advances by Potiphar's wife. (See Genesis 39:1-10.)

If you are always on the defensive with the people around you, you may be around the wrong people. Guarding the anointing has a lot to do with guarding your inner circle.

When Samson exposed his weakness to his love, he was captured and his eyes were gouged out. The enemy desires to strip the oil from you, then blind you, so that you are unable to locate it again. All this was the result of stupidity on Samson's part. He mistakenly put his trust in a person who evidently meant him harm. Never put your trust *in* a person. That type of trust is reserved for God alone.

Once people show you who they are, believe them! Delilah, through her actions, showed her deviant motivations. While Samson was blinded by *eros* (romantic love), she was cheating on him with mammon (wealth). Samson's enemies promised to pay Delilah if she could obtain the secret of his anointing. Revealing his secret hurt more than it helped. In reality, it caused betrayal, loss of vison, and eventually, redemption. Ultimately, the revealing of his secret to Delilah put Samson in position to kill his enemies, but it also cost him his life.

7 Secrets to Guarding Your Anointing

1. *Don't allow your oil to get tainted by prostitution* (see Judg. 16:1). As Samson shared company with a harlot, his enemies were made aware of it. When we're in sin, the devil broadcasts it, spiritually and naturally. Sin will taint your anointing (effectiveness). Guard your anointing by abstaining from the very appearance of evil. If you do fall into sin, true repentance to God will absolve you of your transgression and bring you into right standing with the Lord. It will be as if the sin was never committed at all.

2. *Don't ever allow your anointing to replace your intelligence.* Sometimes we become so reliant on our oil that it trumps our intellect. When we get saved, it shouldn't dumb us down. It should "smarten" us up! The oil will never totally replace the intellect that comes from being in relationship with Jesus Christ, the anointed One.

3. *Keep your head anointed.* Remember the sheep previously referred to? The oil that was poured upon their heads kept the insects from getting into their brains. It's the same with us. The enemy desires to infiltrate our minds, because once he gets in our heads, our bodies follow. By staying "oily," demonic infiltration is less likely.

4. *Don't share the secret to your anointing with everyone.* Everyone is not saved and even if they are,

they may not be for you. There are some people in the body whom you should not share the secret of your oil with because they will use it for your demise. Remember, David stated in Psalm 41:9 that *"Even my close friend, someone I trusted, one who shared my bread, has turned against me"* (NIV).

5. *Don't allow human love to cause you to reveal something God told you to keep secret.* Love can blind you. This is exactly what happened to Samson— literally! Don't allow *pillow talk* to cause you to reveal the secret of your oil. The devil will use your appetite to entrap you and lead you to give away to dogs that which is holy.

6. *When the truth is shared outside of kairos (God's time), it can negatively affect chronos (chronological time).* Just because it is the truth doesn't necessarily mean that it should be shared. It's prudent to wait on the Lord's permission before releasing the secret of your anointing to anyone.

7. *Don't reveal the secret of your oil because it may cost you your vision.* After Samson revealed that his anointing was in his hair and Delilah had it cut off, his enemies came in and blinded him. Samson was first blinded spiritually. He didn't *see* or discern the true nature of Delilah. What happened to him in the natural, first happened in the spirit. Don't suffer the same fate. We must see in the spirit to avoid calamity in the natural.

Live Abundantly in the Freedom God Designed for You!

In order to walk in supernatural deliverance, guarding your anointing is non-negotiable. You never want to give the enemy an opportunity to get into your temple (body). The tools within the chapters of this book you've just read will help you to overcome the obstacles that the devil has placed before you to keep you bound. The Lord wants you to walk in a new level of freedom. He doesn't want you to carry the weight of the aftermath of continuous demonic battering. Instead, He wants you to know your opponent's strategies, tactics, and plans. You can do this through fasting, prayer, and deliverance. This will cause you to walk out your mandate in Him. It will give you 20/20 eyesight in the Spirit.

Your supernatural deliverance must be maintained. I can't emphasize this point enough. This is done by committing yourself to regular deliverance, be it done by others or yourself. This way, your house will be more likely to stay clean (demon-free). Just like the watchman of the Old Testament stood guard in a high tower to see their enemies from afar, we too have to stand watch over our souls. We never want the devil to catch us sleeping on our post. We must remain vigilant when it comes to matters of impending spiritual attack.

If you are living under demonic oppression, it's time to rise up and walk in the supernatural deliverance Jesus purchased for you. I truly believe that this is your season (time) to victoriously engage demons and overcome the forces of darkness at work in your life. When you're supernaturally delivered, you'll experience more joy and liberty in your walk with the Most High. Take hold of your destiny and move into the profound freedom that God planned for you to live.

APPENDIX

SUPERNATURALLY DELIVERED PRAYERS, PROPHECIES, DECREES, AND DIRECTION

As I mentioned in Chapter 11, I firmly believe that prophetic ministry goes hand in hand with deliverance. One of my gifts from God to the body of Christ is the gift of prophecy. Over the course of writing this book, the Lord gave me several categories of prophetic messages to help fortify the deliverance process for you and others who read them. Some of what I will share below may be unconventional, but I believe the Spirit of God is creative and we get the best from Him when we allow Him to do a new thing. I also trust Him—and I pray you do too—to connect you to the right word at the right time, so that your supernatural deliverance comes rushing in like a flood.

I pray that you will allow Him to illuminate exactly what He has for you as you engage with the words, prayers, and declarations below.

Salvation Opens the Door to Supernatural Deliverance

Salvation is the prerequisite to supernatural deliverance. If you don't know Jesus Christ as Lord and Savior, repeat the following sincerely. God will hear you!

Lord Jesus, for too long I've kept You out of my life. I know I am a sinner and I cannot save myself. No longer will I close the door when I hear You knocking. By faith, I gratefully receive Your gift of salvation. I am ready to trust You as my Lord and Savior.

Thank You, Lord Jesus, for coming to earth. I believe You are the Son of God who died on the cross for my sins and rose from the dead on the third day.

Thank You for bearing my sins and giving me the gift of eternal life. I believe Your words are true. Come into my heart, Lord Jesus, and be my Savior. Amen.[1]

If you prayed this prayer, let me be the first to extend a warm welcome into the family of God. As you seek Him for help and direction for your life, pray that He will also continue to lead you toward being delivered from all the traps and entanglements of the enemy, so that you can live the abundant and free life He purchased for you.

SUPERNATURALLY DELIVERED PRAYERS

Prayer for Supernatural Deliverance

Father God, in Jesus's name, I pray for Your deliverance to come now. Lord, at this moment, I submit my body to You as a living sacrifice—wholly and acceptable to be used for Your reasonable service, in Jesus's name.

I come out of agreement with anything spiritually detrimental that has attached itself to me by any means, in Jesus's name. I bind any and all associations through genealogy, biology, proximity, willfulness, influence, or any work of the flesh that has caused demonic entities to attach to me and torment me, in Jesus's name. At this moment, I sever and break every bond in Jesus's name.

Lord, I pray that You will begin to purge me at once, as I come out of agreement with everything that is not like You. I ask that my will be Your will, in Jesus's name.

I thank You that You will cleanse my temple according to Your perfect work in Jesus. I'm thankful for Your wisdom, knowledge, and power that will be manifested through the Holy Spirit and applied to my life immediately to bring forth mighty deliverance.

Father, as I begin to breathe in and breathe out, You are destroying bonds and breaking yokes.

I come out of agreement with every evil spirit, entity, malfeasance, allegiance, occultism, disobedience, anger, hatred, sin, or any negativity that has manifested in my life.

I cancel any soul tie, affliction, and curse, and cast them from my bloodline now, in Jesus's name.

I bind any and all strongholds and demonic influences that have come into my life, in Jesus's name. Father, I ask that You begin to cleanse me and make me whole. I thank You for Psalm 51 that says that the bones You have broken may rejoice.

I thank You for giving me the mind of Christ.

I praise You, Father, for total deliverance and freedom. I speak that my heart shall be turned toward Your heart in this hour. I cancel all demonic assignments over my life and evict and eradicate them from my bloodline.

I thank You for creating me to be strong and to live a life of total freedom from any demonic oppression or influence in Jesus's name.

I thank You for sharpening my spiritual vision and increasing my discernment so that I may sense the areas where I need to pray, specifically for my own deliverance. I thank You for the gift of discernment, that I may see hidden areas where I may be unaware of a demon's influence over me.

I thank You for bringing to my lips the fruit of Your Word that causes these bonds to be broken immediately, in Jesus's name.

I praise You for the act of delivering us just as You delivered the children of Israel and that You have made a way for Your sons and daughters to be free. I receive it wholly right now!

I seal any open doors, portals, or entry points from demonic entities, and cover them with the blood of Jesus. Every entity, demon, and work of evil that previously beset me is bound, in Jesus's name, rendered to the pit, and will never torment me again.

I speak that I am clean and delivered by the blood of the Lamb. I praise and thank You, God, for total freedom, in Jesus's name! Amen.

By Elisa Veal

Prayer Against Demonic Prophecies

Father God, in Jesus's name, I come against every prophetic word that I've ever received that did not originate from You. I ask You to cleanse me of all demonic residue that resulted from receiving those false words. I cancel the assignments of every demonic prophecy that has been spoken over my life, past and present. I renounce any acceptance of those same words and come against the various principalities behind them. Lord, give me discernment to recognize demonic prophetic words! Help me to differentiate the voice that belongs to You from the voice of the enemy! Thank You, Father, for giving me ears to hear, a spirit to discern, and spiritual eyes to see all that You have for me. I will no longer be taken in by the deceptive ways of false prophets, but will hear Your voice warning me not to receive words that weren't spoken by You, in Jesus's name!

Prayer to Detach the Bastard Spirit

Father God, in the name of Jesus, I reject and detach the spirit of the bastard from my life. Lord, please remove every demonic stronghold related to unplanned pregnancy, being misborn, misbegotten, unwanted, unloved, impure, or any other lie of the enemy that has attached itself to me due to being born out of wedlock. I come against the spirits of shame, rejection, low self-esteem, isolation, timidity, low self-worth, loneliness, self-doubt, and any other demonic entities that have made their home in my flesh! Come out now, in the name of Jesus! I claim my freedom, immediately! No longer will I be bound by anything but the Lord! Where He is, there is liberty! I accept the freedom that Jesus purchased for me! No longer will I feel like I was a mistake! Although my parents didn't plan me, God did! Hallelujah! I can feel these evil spirits departing now! The oil of God is being poured on the top of my head, running down to my feet. As the anointing flows over me, devils are slipping off and out of me! I'm being supernaturally delivered right now! (Start giving the Lord praise until your deliverance manifests.)

Prayer to Overcome the Spirit of Rejection

Father God, in the name of Jesus, I come against the spirit of rejection and every demon that's linked to it! I renounce every word spoken or action taken that allowed this spirit to take root in my life. I cancel its claim to my physical body through the sins of my ancestors. Lord, cleanse me of any responsibility connected to the generations before me, and cancel the enemy's assignment on future ones. I thank You that this is being done in Jesus's name now as I'm reciting this prayer. Supernatural deliverance is hitting my family and me like a tsunami, forcing out every evil spirit of rejection! I ask You, Lord, to fortify me and uphold me when it comes to battling this spirit. I ask You to reveal to me just how this spirit gained entry and download strategies for its permanent exit from my body. I come in agreement with Your plans and believe that I will receive self-deliverance from the spirit of rejection by and through this prayer, in Jesus's name! Amen.

Prayer Against Familial Spirits

Father God, in the name of Jesus, I come against every evil spirit that I've inherited, through no fault of my own, through my lineage. These demons were in relatives who passed away and now seek refuge within other members of my family, including me! Devil, you have no place or right to my body, nor anyone else's in my family, in Jesus's name! I revoke any evil spirit previously given access to our family, past and present, in the matchless name of Jesus Christ! I reject any satanic residue that attempts to get on future generations within my family. Your demonic power over us stops here and now! You caused sickness, strife, death, division, divorce, miscarriages, accidents, etc. (name any others) within our family, but no longer! We bind and wage war over every tactic, plan, and strategy of the enemy now! Satan, your familial assignment in my life is cancelled now, in Jesus's name! Glory to God! Amen.

Prayer to Remove Demonic Residue from Cursed Objects

Father God, in the name of Jesus, I ask You to remove any demonic residue left by demons that have exited my person. I ask forgiveness for willfully or unknow- ingly allowing them in through my possession of cursed objects. Lord, I have or am in the process of getting rid of said objects and want no trace of their residue to be upon myself, my family, my home, my vehicle, or anything that belongs to me. I renounce every effect, consequence, or retaliation caused by the residue left by any evil objects that have been in my possession in the past. I thank You, God, for cleansing me of any tainted oil that was left on me by evacuating devils. I have been cleansed by the Blood of the Lamb and His completed work. There is no residue on me, my home, family, vehicle, relatives, pets, or anything that I own, in Jesus's name! I thank You, Lord, for hearing this sincere prayer and cleansing me from all unrighteousness and all demonic oil, in Jesus's wonderful name! Hallelujah! (Note: Praise the Lord until you sense or feel victorious in Him.)

Prayer Against the Spirit of Imbalance

Father God, in the name of Jesus, I come against the spirit of imbalance that comes to throw me out of balance with Your word. Proverbs 11:1 tells me that a false balance is an abomination to You, but a just weight is Your delight. Let me be right, just, and honest in the weight of your righteous balance. Don't allow me to ever counterbalance that which has already been balanced by You. Allow me to discern Your just weight, avoiding the unjust weight of the enemy, which causes discord, strife, and division. God, not only are You just, but You are Justice. You are fair and balanced in all Your ways! I will not allow an evil spirit of imbalance to permeate the divine balance that You give joyfully to Your children, even though they may not always see or use it. Daddy, I thank You for allowing the weight of good to outbalance the weight of evil, continuously. Because of this, the scales of goodness, mercy, and favor will be on my side all the days of my life, in Jesus's name! Amen.

Self-Deliverance Prayer

Father God, in the name of Jesus, show me how to rid myself of all demonic habitation. Give me the name of the strongman (head demon), so that I may cast it out along with the imps or lower-ranking demons attached to him. Help me when there is not a deliverance minister available and I need to rid myself of demons effectively. Allow me to cast them out of my body, in the precious name of Jesus. Don't let fear keep me from doing it. Lord, permit my phobias to be overcome by my faith and assist me in pushing everything that's not of You out of me! Lord, open up a door to give me the privacy to embark on an intimate self-deliverance session, unimpeded by constant interruptions. Give me Your supreme confidence, so that I can rid myself of demons within with power and authority, in the name of Your precious Son. Give me the power and authority to tread on serpents and scorpions, and over all the power of the enemy (Luke 10:19). Let Satan's threats be nullified and empty because of my use of the name of Jesus, whom I have an eternally personal relationship with. As I receive my deliverance, I will walk in a new freedom, feeling a sense of lightness in the absence of the demonic weight that I've carried for years. I call it done in the matchless name of Yeshua Hamashiach (Jesus the Messiah). Amen!

Prayer for the Gift of Discernment

Father God, in the name of Jesus, give me 20/20 vision in the spirit realm. Allow me to discern (perceive) that which cannot be readily seen with the human eye. Lord, let me see demonic activities, strategies, and plans long before they are executed in my life. Father, don't let my spiritual senses become dull. Keep me sharp as a knife in the spirit, so that I can thwart the attacks of the enemy before they transpire. I thank You, Father, that I am able to envision the fiery darts of the devil before they are thrown, resist the enemy before he squeezes, and avoid the pitfalls he maniacally sets before me. I see through Your eyes, so Satan can't catch me by surprise. Through You, I discern his moves and counteract his assaults. Again, thank You for giving me the gift of discernment, in Jesus's name! Amen.

Prayer to Fortify Your Spirit and Body for War

Father God, in the name of Jesus, strengthen both my spirit and my body for war against the enemy of my soul.

Like King David, teach my hands to war and my fingers to fight (Ps. 144:1). Strengthen me to fight the good fight of faith (1 Tim. 6:12). Allow my praise of You to be a weapon against the devil, in the spirit and the natural. I thank You, Lord, that my sincere praise fortifies both my spirit and body against continuous attacks by the hordes of hell! Hallelujah! Glory to Your Holy Name! As I give You praise, I feel lost strength returning to me! I'm putting on the armor that You've supplied me within the book of Ephesians, the sixth chapter, readying myself for battle! No longer will I run from the enemy. Like young David did to Goliath, I will run toward him! Fear will not cause me to faint or to stop being proactive when it comes to engaging the enemy. You being with me is more than a world against me. Of whom will I be afraid? Who will I fear? Lord, You've already made me victorious through Christ Jesus. I've won now, because He won then! I'm fortified by You when it comes to the devil's assaults. I'm ready for war! Amen!

SUPERNATURALLY DELIVERED PROPHECIES

It's time.

I believe it's your season to come out of that which has restricted you. It's time for reality and your dreams to collide. All the effort and hard work you've put in over the years is about to pay off. What looked like a setback served only to stoke the fire of advancement on the inside of you!

You've used previous failures as fuel to get you to the point you're at now. It's time to reach even higher.

It's time to empty yourself so that the Lord can pour more into you.

It's time to strategize for the greater rewards even though your finances dictate otherwise.

It's time for your faith to cause ingenuity to manifest into tangible blessings.

It is your time to take risks and launch out in the direction that Jesus instructs you to. Your nets will burst due to the greatness of your catch.

The spirit of failure attempted to thwart your destiny, but God put the spirit of enduring faith on the inside of you. There's no quit in you!

You've endured the slings and arrows of the enemy. You've praised the Lord even when things didn't go your way. He's collected your tears and has turned them into a deluge of blessings in this season. It's time! Selah.

You bet on the wrong horse!

They counted you out, thinking you were a nobody because you don't have a huge following, a published book, or full traveling itinerary. Instead of pushing you, they pushed the ones who were "more likely to succeed." They didn't recognize what the Lord had placed in you. They didn't see you through the lenses of the Father. You were only visible to them when they could benefit from you. So, they "bet" on another horse that appeared more profitable.

Don't misunderstand me here: I'm not referring to the type of bet in which a wager is placed, but that which is "a person, thing, or action with a (specified) likelihood of achieving success or bringing about a desired result: [for example] 'he's the best bet for the job.'"[2]

So, all their time, energy, and effort were placed on the horse that looked like a winner. This was done because the perception was that you'd reached your maximum potential. They thought that there's no way you could ever win a race. *Why would they bet on you?* they may have thought.

Guess what? They were wrong!

Yes, you were at the end of the pack, but this is your season to surge to the front. You are surging! You are moving faster. God is supernaturally accelerating you. You are going to surpass your expectations and theirs. They made a tremendous error! They bet on the wrong horse when all bets should have been placed on you!

I see you in the winners' circle with a medal being placed around your neck. All your labor, tears, and pain were worth it. You've surpassed the limitations of others. The only true limits were those placed on you by you!

This is your victory season because you ran the race with patience, not selfish ambition. You preferred others above your-self. You truly rejoiced when people were moving ahead faster than you. You blessed your enemies instead of cursing them. You kept quiet when the enemy wanted you to boast. Again, I say, they bet on the wrong horse. They should have bet on you. Selah!

> *Wherefore seeing we also are compassed about with so great a cloud of witnesses, let us lay aside every weight, and the sin which doth so easily beset us, and let us run with patience the race that is set before us, looking unto Jesus the author and finisher of our faith; who for the joy that was set before him endured the cross, despising the shame, and is set down at the right hand of the throne of God* (Hebrews 12:1-2).

This is your season of elevation!

You've been underestimated, overlooked, and counted out by people, but not by God. This is your season to astonish and amaze your doubters!

You are like a train that gathers momentum the longer it runs. You've labored in obscurity, waiting for affirmation from others, when the Lord has already confirmed you. This is the season where He elevates you. God will do it for you. He wants you to realize that your acceleration is due to Him and Him alone.

All the tears you've cried, betrayals you've experienced, and letdowns you've dealt with were fuel for your journey. They kept you pressing forward when in actuality, the devil meant them for your downfall. Because you didn't give up or give in, you're qualified for promotion. Not just a natural advancement, but a supernatural one!

This is your upgrade season!

Humble yourselves therefore under the mighty hand of God, that he may exalt you in due time (1 Peter 5:6).

The word *upgrade* means "to improve, new version of, an increase, enhance."[3] The definition of the word *exalt* is "to raise in rank, power, character, quality, etc.; to praise; extol."[4]

I heard the word *upgrade* for you. This means that it's your season to upgrade some major areas of your life—your thought life, prayer life, praise and worship, and relationships. This is your time to receive a download from heaven that will upgrade all previous "software" purchased with tears during various times of undue suffering.

I hear the Spirit of God saying, "I'm turning your mourning into morning," meaning that your weeping may have lasted for a night, but with the morning comes joy! The joy of the Lord instantaneously transforms into strength, according to Nehemiah 8:10. People may have overlooked and forgotten about you, but God never did!

This is the season when your pain evolves into a fulfilled promise! All that you've gone through has been for a purpose, on purpose! Your steps are ordered. Be encouraged. You're in the midst of an upgrade. With the upgrade comes exaltation (promotion), not just from man but also from God!

You're in position for the push.

This is not the season to let others determine the direction of your destiny with their opinions, criticism, and attacks. Don't rely on people to *blow* into your purpose. Do not be afraid to be who God has called you to be. A prophetic wind that previously blew over you has repositioned itself behind you. It's begun to push you into His purpose, like a giant hand placed upon your back. This wind is the very breath of God.

The enemy has longed to prevent this from happening, but it's God's ordained time for it to happen now.

Years ago, you misidentified this push, thinking it was human in scope and origin. Even then, it was the Lord trying to move you, but He needed a yes from you. You resisted the push then, but you won't now. This is literally and spiritually your second wind! You've answered yes to the push.

This push will propel you into greater dimensions and higher heights. The book that you've been pregnant with will be pushed out! The ministry that's in your belly will be pushed out! The business that is in you will be pushed out!

You are in the correct position for the push. Allow the wind of God to take you in the way He wants you to go! This is the season to permit God to push you. This is your moment of movement. Push!

Break ground and come forth!

> *Break up your unplowed* [fallow] *ground and do not sow among thorns. Circumcise yourselves to the Lord, circumcise your hearts, you people of Judah and inhabitants of Jerusalem* (Jeremiah 4:3-4, NIV).

According to First Chronicles 12:32, the children of Issachar were men who understood times (seasons) and were able to know what Israel should do. I believe that these types of prophets exist now and can speak as oracles of God, so that we may be provided with divine direction. Some things we hear come from a fleshy or sensual place instead of the Holy Spirit.

Is it a word from the Lord?

At the beginning of each year or new season in God, there's a great tendency for some in the body of Christ to create catchy slogans or appealing rhythmical catch phrases, such as, "God told me you'll be fine in 2009," "It's going to be great in 2008," or "It's going to be heaven in 2007!"

I used to go along with numerous such sayings. I swiftly discovered, through experiencing adverse situations contrary to said mottos, that many did not originate from the Lord. This led me to continuously ask Him what was on His heart and mind for the next season. I routinely do this in December, sometimes a couple of months earlier.

> *Sow for yourselves righteousness, reap the fruit of steadfast love; break up your fallow ground, for it is the time to seek the Lord, that he may come and rain salvation upon you* (Hosea 10:12, RSV).

A flower in the middle of a sidewalk.

Have you ever seen a flower growing in the middle of a sidewalk? I have. I've always contemplated the strength, tenacity, and perseverance it must have taken it to accomplish such an arduous task. I tossed around the idea of its gestation period in retrospect to the plant's emergence through inches of solid concrete. Despite the hardness of the cement, it broke through! I associate the plight of the flower to some of you who are reading this right now. I prophesy that it's your season to break up ground and come forth!

Come forth!

In order to come forth, you must break ground. The prerequisite is that it must be fallow. Fallow (or inactive) ground is customarily "cultivated land that is allowed to lie idle during the growing season."[5] In other scenarios, it is unplowed ground that refuses to allow crops to grow. It is land that could be productive, but, for whatever reason, has not been broken up, tilled, plowed, and prepared for planting. In its current state, it's unusable, much like the stony ground that Jesus spoke about in Matthew 13.

In your current state, it appears, on the surface, that there's no way the Lord could use you. When you look at your fallow or unplowed land, your first thought would probably be, "There's no way that this land could produce anything!" But looks can be deceiving!

Many judge the ground by its surface, not realizing what's happening beneath it. Some thought you wouldn't come forth based on how your situation looks now. They don't realize that what looks like a permanent condition is not.

Some of you have labored in obscurity and darkness for years. There were few who realized what you were doing or who you were. Breaking ground will cause you to break through the covers that hid you, permitting the glory of God to shine through so others can find or see you.

For all that is secret will eventually be brought into the open, and everything that is concealed will be brought to light and made known to all (Luke 8:17, NLT).

You were kept in secret and guarded for years, but this will be your season to debut in Him. Mind you, the Lord has always known you and your mandate, but He strategically kept it and you hidden from those who couldn't handle who He's called you to be.

Season of the groundbreakers.

Groundbreakers, now is your time! It's ideal to break up fallow ground now in preparation to plant new seed. Furthermore, I sense a sound, a shift, and a shaking up, due to the breaking up of fallow ground. Old things will be dislodged and disrupted in order to solidify and lodge the new. In order for novel things to come forth, you must break ground. To come forth, you have to fracture the fallow, unproductive ground.

Keep plowing.

Keep plowing; keep working! When Elisha was initially mantled by Prophet Elijah in First Kings 19, He was working with twelve yokes of oxen. Elijah literally threw his coat (mantle) upon him while Elisha was plowing. The work and the mandate always come before the mantling.

You have been doing the work of ministry. Now, you're being mantled in order to come forth in this next season. Your land (ministry) was allowed to be fallow (unusable) so that it could be fruitful (useable) in the days and months to come.

Sometimes you have to be broken down in order to break through.

Oftentimes, we must first be broken down by the actions of others and then rebuilt by God. When you're reconstructed by the Lord, you become even stronger than before—strong enough to break through because you were built again by the God of the breakthrough (*Baal-perazim*; see 1 Chron. 14:10-11).

Don't use prayer as an excuse!

There are numerous times when we receive answers from God, but we're so busy talking that we don't take the time to listen to Him. How can we know His will if we never incline our ears to His voice? Even worse, how can we hear Him without knowing His voice? The reason some don't see their requests being fulfilled is because prayer was used as an excuse not to work their faith. Faith without works is dead (see James 2:17). In order to break up ground, you must put legs on your faith!

There are times when we shouldn't continue praying the same prayers; we should act on them. A prime example is when Moses and the children of Israel were about to cross the Red Sea. The Egyptians were in hot pursuit. The Israelites began to direct their complaints toward Moses. He, in turn, began to pray to God. The Lord responded with a rebuke, "Why are you crying out to me? Tell the Israelites to move on" (Exod. 14:15 NIV).

4 WAYS TO BREAK UP THE FALLOW GROUND

1. Do not sow seed among thorns. Thorns represent anything that hinders your growth. It's the enemy of your seed.

2. Clear your heart of weeds. When you look at the ground that appears barren, weeds of bitterness can grow in your heart!

3. Don't be afraid of work.

4. Subtract everything in your life that steals from your seed.

SUPERNATURALLY DELIVERED DAILY DECREES

I AM

I am supernaturally delivered.

I am a supernatural deliverer.

I am free from oppression.

I am free from depression.

I am no longer bound by the enemy.

I am above only and not beneath.

I am who the Lord says I am.

I am a believer.

I am an overcomer.

I am a groundbreaker.

I am a minister of deliverance.

I am not bound by my past.

I am not cursed.

I am not stressed.

I am blessed.

I am anointed and appointed.

I am equipped for war.

I Have the Authority of a Believer

As a believer in Jesus Christ, I have authority and power over Satan.

I walk in the authority of a believer in Jesus Christ!

I have power and authority over every plan, strategy, or set-up by the enemy, in Jesus's name.

I win every major battle against Satan because of Jesus's finished work at the cross.

The devil is a defeated foe in my life, having only the power that I give him.

As a believer, I have the ability to tread on serpents and scorpions (Luke 10:19).

As a believer, nothing shall by any means hurt me.

Satan can't do anything to me that God doesn't allow.

I continuously walk in the victory of Christ even before problems manifest.

I call those things that be not as though they were (Romans 4:17).

Permission Denied!

I retract any permission given to demons to wreak havoc in my life.

I withdraw permission granted to Satan by my ancestors, giving access to me, my family, and offspring.

I deny entry, access, influence, and authority to any evil spirits over my body.

I renounce all previously given permission to Satan through sins committed in my past.

I repent of any sin that gave the enemy access to my body, in Jesus's name.

Satan does not have permission to afflict me with sickness.

Poverty does not have my permission to come into my life to stay.

The spirit of fear does not have my permission to live in me!

Doubt does not have my permission to hinder my faith.

Access is denied to anything that will prevent me from being supernaturally delivered!

Don't Talk to Strangers!

I will not entertain foreign voices of demonic origin, naturally or spiritually (Deuteronomy 27:10).

I refuse to have ongoing dialogue with demons (Luke 4:33-35).

I won't make a series of inquiries to demons because they are liars (John 8:44).

I will not respond when Satan asks me questions because I know his schemes (2 Corinthians 2:11).

I will listen to the voice of God and follow it! (John 10:27).

I will study to be quiet (1 Thessalonians 4:11).

I will not abandon the faith and listen to evil deceptions or instructions from demons (1 Timothy 4:1).

I will not engage or interact with familiar spirits.

I do not desire to engage in any communications, except for those conveyed through the Holy Spirit.

I repent for any past, present or future extended conversations with devils.

I Will Guard My Anointing

I will be overly protective of the oil upon my life.

Unlike Samson, I will not divulge the secret of my anointing to Delilah (any person plotting my destruction for gain) (Proverbs 11:13).

The glory of the Lord will be my rear guard (Isaiah 58:8).

I will guard my heart at all times (Proverbs 4:23).

I paid a price for the oil on my life.

My anointing causes me to be effective.

I receive the oil of the Lord.

I value and cherish my anointing, knowing that it came from the hand of God.

My anointing positions me for victory in the Lord's Kingdom.

The anointing that I carry is powerful!

I Denounce Demonic Marriages

I will not be a husband/bride of any evil spirit in hell.

I divorce any demon who has ever claimed me as its spouse.

I annul, abort, nullify, and void any demons produced by this unholy union.

I come against any residue left upon me from any and every demonic encounter.

I break every ungodly soul tie established through any and every unholy union.

I cancel any commitment made over my life to any demonic coupling.

I bind any demons trying to infiltrate my marriage to render it demonic.

I rescind any demonic vow that I have ever spoken.

I will not be partnered, brokered, or joined to any demonic entity attached to my lineage.

My marriage will be blessed, anointed by God, no demon will be allowed entry.

Cleaning My House!

I will do a spiritual cleaning of my house, getting rid of everything that's not of God.

The Lord will show me any demonic objects in my home that need to be destroyed.

I will anoint my doors, windows, bedposts, furniture, and other possessions with holy, blessed oil.

I will make divine decisions concerning what I bring into my home from now on.

I will allow anointed music and/or the Word of the Lord (Bible) to play softly in my house 24 hours a day.

I rule my house (1 Timothy 3:5).

My house is built by wisdom (Proverbs 24:3).

I command the fire of God to cleanse and purify my home of every spirit that is not like Him.

My home is swept and garnished, prepared for the Master's use.

I command every open portal or doorway in my home to be closed now, in Jesus's name.

I dedicate my home to God and invite Him to take residence.

Shutting Demonic Doors

I cast the demonic strongman (identify him) out of myself, in Jesus's name.

Lord, give me discernment to identify demonic doors.

Grant me supernatural vision to perceive godly doors, and the power to walk through them.

I shut every demonic door that I have ever opened in the past.

God, give me the wisdom, willpower, and fortitude to not open and go through the doors the enemy provides.

I withdraw any access granted to demons to the door of my body (temple).

I command any door that was opened by anyone in my bloodline to be shut and sealed by the power of God.

I proclaim supernatural strength to spiritually close every demonic door.

I cast every demon out in Jesus's name, and seal every door and entry point.

Lord, appoint an angelic gatekeeper over every door in Jesus's name.

I Will Walk in Divine Wholeness

By His stripes, I am healed (Isaiah 53:5).

I am healed of backsliding (Hosea 14:4).

The Lord will bring me to health and healing (Jeremiah 33:6).

My healing will happen quickly (Isaiah 58:8).

If I am ever sick, God will sustain me (Psalm 41:3).

The Lord will heal my flesh and strengthen my bones (Proverbs 3:7-8).

I will serve the Lord and He will take sickness away from me (Exodus 23:25).

The Lord will satisfy me with long life (Psalm 91:16).

I cried out and the Lord healed me (Psalm 30:2).

He sent His word and healed me (Psalm 107:20).

My body is healthy and strong (Psalm 73:5)!

The Lord has healed my broken heart (Psalm 147:3).

The Lord has restored me and caused me to live (Isaiah 38:16)!

God delivers me from all my afflictions (Psalm 34:19).

He has supernaturally delivered my soul in peace (Psalm 55:18).

God is the health of my countenance (Psalm 42:11).

Pleasant words are sweet to my soul and health to my bones (Proverbs 16:24).

The Lord heals me when my bones are vexed (Psalm 6:2).

God strengthens my heart as I wait upon Him (Psalm 27:14).

The peace of God keeps (guards) my heart and mind (Philippians 4:7).

The prayer of faith saves me from sickness (James 5:15).

God did not give me a spirit of fear! (2 Timothy 1:7)

I am prosperous and in health (3 John 1:2).

SUPERNATURALLY DELIVERED DIRECTION— DID GOD TELL YOU TO MOVE THERE?

This I say then, Walk in the Spirit, and ye shall not fulfil the lust of the flesh (Galatians 5:16).

As I was driving one day, I heard that each city in America has a personality. *Personality* is defined as "the quality (moods or habits) that makes one different from others."⁶ Philadelphia is known as loving. New York's personality is said to be curious, intellectual, and creative. These are just a few examples of the humanistic qualities a city may have.

Now, there are principalities with personalities that rule most cities. They are identified by the monuments erected that give homage to the false gods that they represent. If you look at the structure of a building, what do you see as you look past the physical design? What registers in your spirit?

There are demonic strongholds in some cities with distinct personalities and character. There are demonic watchmen in those cities seated on towers, that warn the principalities of possible infiltration by true men and women of God. This is one reason some go through so much when they move. It's good practice to inquire of God before moving to a particular city. Don't be led by the flesh; be led by the Spirit.

Have you ever wondered why you're not prospering in a particular city? If you have, check out your city's personality. Identify the city's supernatural rulers that exist in high places, so that you know what you're up against. You never know how your geographic location may play into whether or not you walk fully in supernatural deliverance. If you feel as if you are contending with the demonic personality of the city you live in, seek out the word of the Lord for yourself concerning this matter. Ask Him for a strategy to overcome that spirit's influence in your life.

ENDNOTES

Introduction
Supernatural Deliverance Is Yours!

1. John Veal, *Supernaturally Prophetic* (Shippensburg, PA: Destiny Image, 2018).
2. Merriam-Webster.com, s.v. "supernatural," https://www.merriam-webster.com/dictionary/supernatural.
3. Ivory Hopkins, *Spiritual Warfare Training Manual Revisited* (N.p.: CreateSpace, 2017).

Chapter 1
Seeds of Rejection

1. King James Online Dictionary, s.v. "bastard," as quoted in Webster's 1828 Dictionary, http://www.kingjamesbibledictionary.com/Dictionary/bastard.
2. King James Online Dictionary, s.v. "reject," http://www.kingjamesbibledictionary.com/Dictionary/reject.
3. KJV Bible Dictionary, s.v. "discern," https://av1611.com/kjbp/kjv-dictionary/discern.html.

CHAPTER 2
CHICAGO HORROR STORY

1. Dictionary.com, s.v. "Ouija," https://www.dictionary.com/browse/ouija.
2. Romajidesu.com, s.v. "ouija," http://www.romajidesu.com/dictionary/meaning-of-ouija.html.
3. Dictionary.com, s.v. "Ouija," https://www.dictionary.com/browse/ouija.
4. Wikipedia.com, s.v. "ouija," https://en.wikipedia.org/wiki/Ouija.
5. "The Ouija Board: Just a Game?" Christian Answers for the New Age, http://www.christiananswersforthenewage.org/Articles _OuijaBoard.html.
6. "Who Was the Canaanite God Molech?" Compelling Truth, https://www.compellingtruth.org/molech.html.
7. *Ghostbusters*, directed by Paul Feig, (2016; Los Angeles, CA: Columbia Pictures Corporation).
8. King James Online Dictionary, s.v. "subtil," http://kingjamesbibledictionary.com/Dictionary/subtil.
9. Name withheld, Facebook.com, December 14, 2012.

CHAPTER 3
THERE'S SOMETHING IN MY HOUSE!

1. King James Online Dictionary, s.v. "spirit," http://www .kingjamesbibledictionary.com/Dictionary/spirit.
2. *The Twilight Zone*, episode 19, "The Hunt," directed by Harold Schuster, written by Earl Hamner and Rod Serling, aired January 26, 1962.

CHAPTER 4
PERMISSION GRANTED

1. OxfordDictionaries.com, s.v. "omission," https://en .oxforddictionaries.com/definition/omission.

2. OxfordDictionaries.com, s.v. "commission," https://en.oxforddictionaries.com/definition/us/COMMISSION.

3. "Understanding Cancer: Statistics," National Cancer Institute, https://www.cancer.gov/about-cancer/understanding/statistics, April 27, 2018.

4. Biblehub.com, s.v. "pheugo," https://biblehub.com/greek/5343.htm.

Chapter 5
Here to Destroy

1. OxfordDictionaries.com, s.v. "disclaimer," https://en.oxforddictionaries.com/definition/disclaimer.

Chapter 6
Unclean Spirits and Cursed Objects: Books

1. KJV Bible Dictionary, s.v. "unclean," http://av1611.com/kjbp/kjv-dictionary/unclean.html.

2. OxfordDictionaries.com, s.v. "foul," https://en.oxforddictionaries.com/definition/foul.

3. Lester Frank Sumrall, *101 Questions and Answers on Demon Powers* (N.p.: Sumrall Publishing, 1999).

Chapter 7
Unclean Spirits and Cursed Objects: Sin in the Camp

1. The Meaning of the Name, s.v. "Achan," https://themeaningofthename.com/achan/.

2. Biblegateway.com, s.v. "1 Chronicles 2:7," https://www.biblegateway.com/passage/?search=1%20Chronicles+2:7&version=NLT.

3. Webopedia.com, s.v. "Trojan horse," https://www.webopedia.com/TERM/T/Trojan_horse.html.

4. Merriam-Webster.com, s.v. "idol," https://www.merriam-webster.com/dictionary/idol.

CHAPTER 9
SELF-DELIVERANCE

1. Frank and Ida Mae Hammond, *Pigs in the Parlor* (Kirkwood, MO: Impact Christian Books, 1973).
2. Ruth Brown, *Destroying the Works of Witchcraft through Fasting and Prayer* (N.p.: Impact Christian Books, 1994).

CHAPTER 10
DELIVERANCE 101: THE BASICS

1. Bible.hub.com, s.v. "peletah," https://biblehub.com/hebrew/6413.htm.
2. Merriam-Webster.com, s.v. "deliver," https://www.merriam-webster.com/dictionary/deliver.
3. Merriam-Webster.com, s.v. "house," https://www.merriam-webster.com/dictionary/house.
4. Wikipedia.com, s.v. "Vlad the Impaler," https://en.wikipedia.org/wiki/Vlad_the_Impaler.

CHAPTER 11
DELIVERANCE 101:
DON'T TALK TO STRANGERS

1. Merriam-Webster.com, s.v. "replenish," https://www.merriam-webster.com/dictionary/replenish.

CHAPTER 12
HEALING, DELIVERANCE, AND THE PROPHETIC

1. Merriam-Webster.com, s.v. "wholeness," https://www.merriam-webster.com/thesaurus/wholeness.
2. Ibid.
3. Dictionary.com, s.v. "efficient," https://www.dictionary.com/browse/efficient.

Conclusion
Protect Your Oil

1. Merriam-Webster.com, s.v. "anoint," https://www.merriam-webster.com/dictionary/anoint.
2. Janton, "Anointing Sheep with Oil," Busy.org, https://busy.org/@janton/anointing-sheep-with-oil.

Appendix
Supernaturally Delivered Prayers, Prophecies, Decrees, and Direction

1. "The Sinner's Prayer (by Dr. Ray Pritchard)," Crosswalk.com, February 16, 2017, https://www.crosswalk.com/faith/prayer/prayers/the-sinners-prayer-4-examples.html.
2. YourDictionary.com, s.v. "bet," https://www.yourdictionary.com/bet.
3. Dictionary.com, s.v. "upgrade," https://www.dictionary.com/browse/upgrade?s=t.
4. Dictionary.com, s.v. "exalt," https://www.dictionary.com/browse/exalt.
5. Merriam-Webster.com, s.v. "fallow," https://www.merriam-webster.com/dictionary/fallow.
6. Merriam-Webster.com, s.v. "personality," https://www.merriam-webster.com/dictionary/personality.

ABOUT DR. JOHN VEAL

Dr. John Veal is the senior pastor/prophet of Enduring Faith Christian Center and the CEO of John Veal Ministries Inc. He is passionate about pursuing God's mandate to preach, teach, impart, and activate people within the prophetic.

John is a regular contributor to *Charisma* online magazine, The Elijah List, IMAG, and others. John is also the author of *Supernaturally Prophetic*. He has been featured on various media outlets and is a highly sought-after conference speaker due to his uncanny prophetic accuracy, humor, candor, and unconventional preaching style.

He has traveled the nations, presenting a myriad of prophetic training and ministry. John currently resides in Chicago, Illinois, with his wife, Elisa, and their three children.

JOHN WOULD LOVE TO HEAR FROM YOU

If you would like to learn more about John's ministry or contact him, visit his website at Johnveal.org or his church's website at www.faith2endure.com. There, you can keep up with his schedule and find out where he will be speaking.

You can also reach out to him by mail:

Enduring Faith Christian Center
PO Box 19536
Chicago, IL 60619

For booking information,
please visit www.johnveal.org/bookings/.

If this book has been a blessing to you, please write a review of it at www.Amazon.com. You can also find out more information about this book by visiting www.supernaturallydelivered.com or by contacting us at supernaturallydelivered@gmail.com.

FOLLOW JOHN ONLINE

Facebook: @prophetjv

Twitter: @pastorveal

Instagram: @prophetjohnveal